HANDCRAFT CENTERS
OF NEW ENGLAND

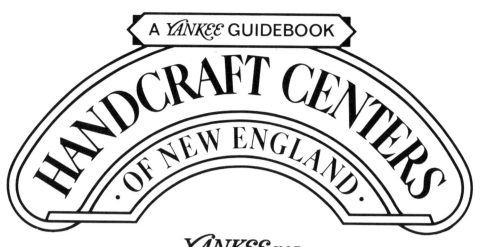

A *YANKEE* GUIDEBOOK

HANDCRAFT CENTERS

· OF NEW ENGLAND ·

YANKEE, INC.
Dublin, New Hampshire

Book design by Bob Orlando
Cover by Rex Peteet

Yankee, Inc., Dublin, New Hampshire 03444
First Edition
Second Printing, 1982
Copyright 1981, by Yankee, Inc.
Printed in the United States of America

Library of Congress Catalog Card No. 80-85481
ISBN 0-911658-26-2

A *YANKEE* GUIDEBOOK

HANDCRAFT CENTERS
OF NEW ENGLAND

Contents

Introduction

This isn't the kind of book you read from cover to cover. It's a guide-book, to be dipped into again and again, with new discoveries to be found every time. But in order to make those discoveries, there are a few things you should know about this book.

1. Addresses and Directions. The address given immediately after the shop/event name is its physical location; when another address is listed in parentheses, that's the mailing address only. (It's not unheard-of in rural New England for a shop to be located in Cornish, New Hampshire, and to have a mailing address in Windsor, Vermont!) Also, where the location is listed as a street and the driving directions give a route number (or vice versa), we haven't lost our minds; the two are one in the same. We've listed both for your convenience in finding these locations on highway signs and maps.

2. Hours. Don't expect studio owners to keep rigid hours. Part of their business involves attending crafts shows, and part of their reason for choosing this lifestyle is that it allows flexible hours. You'll generally find them quite accommodating if they know you're interested in their work — just be sure to call ahead if you're going to be driving any distance. A telephone call in the pre-Christmas season will often reveal extended December hours, and at any time of year a craftsperson whose shop/studio is listed as having hours "by appointment only" will greatly appreciate your cooperation.

3. Terminology. "Daily" is used here to mean "seven days a week." All events take place annually unless otherwise noted.

4. Sources. All information was supplied by shops, studio owners, and event sponsors; it was correct at press time, but of course is subject to change.

5. Omissions. Excluded from this book are shops that have been in business in the same town for less than one year, and craftspeople who work on commission only. Otherwise, every effort has been made to include the best handcrafts New England has to offer. If you discover an outstanding shop, studio, or annual event we've missed, we'd love to hear about it. Just write to: Crafts Editor, Yankee Books, Main Street, Dublin, NH 03444.

That should be all the guidance you need. What follows is a goldmine of New England crafts — we hope you'll enjoy it.

The Editors

I.
Connecticut

Connecticut is the center for crafts *cooperatives* in New England; here, in addition to numerous individual crafts shops and studios, you'll find such enterprises as the Farmington Valley Arts Center in Avon, the Silvermine Guild of Artists in New Canaan, and Bittersweet Farm in Branford. In addition to selling works that are generally of exceptionally high quality, each of these cooperatives offers two other major advantages to the shopper: the chance to meet the artists and artisans in the process of creating their works, and the opportunity to visit a number of professional craftspeople within a fairly small area; instead of driving fifty miles from the leatherworker's shop to the weaver's studio, you just walk five feet.

The only disadvantage to these setups is that the hours maintained by the individual studios within a complex often vary from one craftsperson to the next, and sometimes are fairly loose. You'll usually find at least some of the studios open, but it can be frustrating to arrive at a studio just as the artist is leaving for a crafts fair. So do phone ahead to be sure he'll be in; the worst that can happen is that you'll discover another great crafts show!

Glass vase by Josh Simpson, The Elements Gallery, Greenwich

AVON

Farmington Valley Arts Center, Avon Park North (Box 220), 06001. Professional. Gallery and art center feature the work of about seventeen craftspeople and artists creating stained glass, pottery, leather goods, woodcarvings, jewelry, weavings, and fabric designs. Many artisans operate studios on the premises.

Office open all year, Monday through Friday 9 to 5, Saturday 11 to 4, Sunday 1 to 4; gallery open all year, Tuesday through Saturday 11 to 4, Sunday 1 to 4. Studio hours vary with individual artisans. **Directions:** Take Interstate 84 west exit 39, then follow Route 4 west to Route 10. Take Route 10 north (toward Avon) to Route 44, then turn left onto Route 44. Follow Route 44 approximately 2 miles; after crossing the railroad tracks and passing Feron's Tennis Shop on the right, turn right into Avon Park North and follow signs. (203) 678-1867.

Stoneware pitcher by Mary Barringer, Farmington Valley Arts Center, Avon

BERLIN

Berlin Crafts Expo and Connecticut Crafts Expo, Berlin Fairgrounds, Route 72. A pair of 3-day juried crafts shows, sponsored by American Crafts Expositions, Inc. (Box 368, Canton, 06019) and held the first weekend in June and the last weekend in August. Hours: Friday noon to 7, Saturday and Sunday from 10. Approximately 250 professional artisans from throughout the United States are in attendance, with continuous crafts demonstrations and performing arts stage productions. Food available. 25,000 visitors annually. Admission charge for adults; no charge for children accompanied by parents. **Directions:** Take Interstate 84 exit 27 to Route 66. Follow Route 66 east to the Berlin Turnpike, then head north. Route 72 is off the Berlin Turnpike; follow signs to the fairgrounds. Or, take Interstate 91 exit 16, then head north on Route 15 (which becomes the Berlin Turnpike). (203) 693-6311.

BETHEL

The Hang Up ... a Craft Gallery, 222 Greenwood Avenue, 06801. Professional. Gallery features handcrafted wall decorations such as one-of-a-kind silk batiks, wood mobiles, and wall hangings. Also functional and decorative pottery, lamps, and wind chimes. Prices range from $1.50 to $250. "Our displays enhance the beauty of each product."

Open September through December, Monday through Saturday 10 to 5:30, Sunday 1 to 5; January through August, Tuesday through Saturday 10 to 5:30. **Directions:** From Interstate 84 in Danbury, head southeast on Route 53 to Route 302. Follow Route 302 east to

Bethel. Greenwood Avenue is the main street in town. (203) 748-1055.

BLOOMFIELD

Nel Design Leathers, 106 Woodland Avenue, 06002. Professional. Owner Nancy E. Lagan specializes in leather wallets, portfolios, handbags, attaché cases, and deer-suede shirts. All work is hand traced and hand cut, with appliqués designed to fit each piece. Design, technique, and individualism are stressed. Prices range from $40 to $185.

Open by appointment only; please call. (203) 242-9381.

To get to Branford and Bittersweet Farm, take Interstate 95 exit 56 or 57. The crafts complex is located on Route 1, between these two exits.

BRANFORD

Bittersweet Farm Arts and Crafts Festival, 779 East Main Street. 2-day juried event sponsored by Bittersweet Farm (06405) and held during the Fourth of July weekend. Hours: Saturday and Sunday 10 to 6. Approximately 100 professionals and amateurs exhibit crafts in many media, and fine arts. Some crafts are demonstrated. Restaurant on the premises. 10,000 visitors annually. Admission free. (203) 481-0080.

Bittersweet Farm Creative Arts Village, 779 East Main Street, 06405. Professional and amateur. Housed on a former chicken farm where organic vegetables and Christmas trees are still grown, the village includes eight shops featuring many kinds of gifts and collectibles including cards, books, and herbs. Also in residence are forty craftspeople creating jewelry, leather goods, wood products, metal sculpture, miniature furniture, silk-screened items, children's clothing, pottery, shearling items, paintings, and ship models. Restaurant on the premises.

Open all year: shops and studios open Tuesday through Saturday 11 to 5, Sunday from noon. (Shop and studio hours may vary, however; please call ahead.) (203) 481-0080.

BRIDGEPORT

Goody Knapp's Fine Crafts and Studio, 3010 Fairfield Avenue, 06605. Professional. Selections include pottery, weavings, baskets, jewelry, stained glass, fabric crafts, wood, batik, quilts, hand-woven pillows and rugs, and dolls. Prices range from $1.75 to $300.

Open all year, Monday through Saturday 9:30 to 5:30. **Directions:** Take Interstate 95 east exit 25, then go left at the end of the ramp and continue straight. The studio is on the right, near the fourth traffic light. (203) 368-0174.

BRISTOL

Quilting by Maryann, 56 Morris Avenue, 06010. Professional. Studio specializes in all sizes of quilts, with a variety of patterns. Prices range from $1.50 to $300.

Open by appointment only; please call. (203) 584-2493.

BROADBROOK

R and J Woodcrafts, 60 Graham Road (RFD 1), 06016. Professional. Shop specializes in wood products. Over three hundred items are featured, each "original in design and totally hand crafted." Prices range from $9 to $60.

Open all year, by appointment only; please call. (203) 644-8666.

BROOKFIELD

Aufrichtig's Pottery and Jewelry Shop, 837 Federal Road, 06804. Professional. Shop specializes in handcrafted functional stoneware and porcelain by Norman and Danna Aufrichtig. Items include planters, full dinnerware sets, cutout lamps, and candle holders. Jewelry sold is the work of about twenty-four jewelers and includes many one-of-a-kind pieces. Prices range from $5 to $250. The shop is in a Victorian home.

Open all year, Monday through Friday 10 to 5:30, Saturday to 5. **Directions:** Take Interstate 84 exit 7; turn right at the end of the exit and go straight (north) on Federal Road (Route 7) for ¾ mile. The shop is on the right, about 100 yards beyond the junction with Route 25. (203) 775-0105.

BURLINGTON

Glassworks, 1501 Jerome Avenue (RFD 3), 06013. Professional and amateur. Shop specializes in finished stained glass. Custom orders accepted. Prices range from 50¢ to $500.

Open September through May, Tuesday through Saturday 10 to 5; June through August, Tuesday through Friday 10 to 5, and also by appointment. **Directions:** Take Interstate 84 exit 39, and follow Route 4 west into Burlington. Or, take Interstate 84 to Route 72 west through Bristol, then head north on Route 69. (203) 582-0830.

CANTERBURY

Souk Shen Patchwork, Riverview Drive (RFD 2, Box 3), 06331. Professional. Shop features the works of

Portion of a quilt, Souk Shen Patchwork, Canterbury

Jimmi and Fran Van Keuren, who make patchwork quilts, both tied and hand quilted, using 100% cotton in traditional patterns. Prices range from $150 to $600.

Open all year, by appointment only; please call. (203) 546-9831.

CANTON

Calico Mouse Gift Shop, Route 44, Canton village, 06019. Professional and amateur. Shop specializes in hand-crafted mice, which do everything from play tennis to bake pies. Also carries patchwork pillows, baby items, kitchen accessories, and Christmas decorations. Custom orders accepted. Prices range from $1 to $50.

Open all year, Monday through Saturday 10 to 4; plus open November and December, Sunday 1 to 4. **Directions:** Take Interstate 84 or 91 to Hartford, then follow Route 44 west (becomes Route 202), through Avon to Canton. Or, take Route 8 north to Torrington, and head east on Route 202 to Canton. (203) 693-6048.

Kissing ball, Calico Mouse Gift Shop, Canton

CHESHIRE

Lowe Bow Originals, 1216 Wolf Hill Road, 06410. Professional. Husband-and-wife team Don and Ann Lowe specialize in hand-crafted men's and women's neckwear, working with fabrics from all over the world. Also available are batik ties, in which the Lowes use a newly developed soft color dye. Items cost $4 to $8.50 and up.

Open all year, by appointment only; please call. (203) 272-6172.

Potpourri Peddlers Shoppe, Watch Factory Shoppes, 06410. Professional and amateur. Selections include hand-painted wooden ware and slate, hand-carved wooden boxes, stained-glass planters and mirrors, plus many more items from several hundred craftspeople throughout the United States. Prices range from $3 to $250. Crafts are mostly traditional early American. The shop is located in a restored nineteenth-century watch factory that also houses seventeen other specialty shops. All items for sale have been juried.

To get to Cheshire, take the Wilbur Cross Parkway to Route 10 or routes 68 and 70.

Open January to Thanksgiving, Monday through Saturday 10 to 5:30 (plus open Friday to 8:30), Sunday noon to 5; day after Thanksgiving to Christmas, Monday through Friday 10 to 8:30, Saturday to 5:30, Sunday noon to 5. **Directions:** The shop is located in the center of town, across from Cheshire Academy. (203) 272-0182.

CORNWALL BRIDGE

Cornwall Bridge Pottery, Route 7, 06754. Professional. Features hand-thrown and wood-fired functional pottery. Prices range from 50¢ to $100.

Open all year, daily 9 to 5. **Directions:** Take Route 8 north to Torrington, then head west on Route 4 to Route 7 in Cornwall Bridge; follow Route 7 south about ½ mile. Or, take Interstate 84 exit for Route 7 (near Danbury), and head north. (203) 672-6545.

COVENTRY

Red Goose Farm, Goose Lane, 06238. Professional and amateur. Shop specializes in Victorian lace needlework such as handmade eyelet, cut work, drawn work, pulled thread, fillet netting and knotting, and battenburg tatting. Special attention is paid to the "antique bridal corner."

Open all year, Saturday and Sunday 10 to 5, weekdays by appointment. **Directions:** Take Interstate 86 exit 99 to Route 195. Head south on Route 195 about ¼ mile to the gasoline station, and then turn onto Goose Lane. Red Goose Farm is 3 miles ahead; the shop is in the barn. (203) 742-9137.

CROMWELL

To get to Cromwell, take Interstate 91 exit 21, then follow Route 72 southeast.

Chips n' Chunks, 27 Brittany Circle, 06416. Professional. Shop owner-craftsman John Croasdale specializes in woodcarvings of ducks, geese, and other birds. Other items include bird carvings on clocks, and coffee tables with relief carvings. Prices range from $10 to $400. Croasdale emphasizes "my own particular style of using burned wood for grain effects."

Open all year, evenings 5 to 10. **Directions:** From Interstate 91 exit 21, follow Route 72 for 4 miles, then turn left onto Washington. Go ¼ mile on Washington, then turn onto Evergreen, go ½ mile to Chelsea, and turn right. Brittany Circle is 100 yards ahead, on the left; watch for mailbox. (203) 635-3487.

Roberts Art Studio, 66 Pasco Hill Road, 06416. Professional. Studio features the woodcarvings of Robert L. Bellavia. Selections include clocks, wall plaques, lamps, and tables. Almost all pieces are etched with original designs. Custom orders for signs accepted. Prices range from $30 to $500.

Open all year, daily 10 to 6; please call ahead. **Directions:** From Interstate 91 exit 21, turn right onto Route 72 and go 1 mile to the traffic light (Main Street, East Berlin). Turn right onto Main Street and follow it to the end, then turn right onto Berlin Street. After you cross the bridge, the studio is in the first house on the left. (203) 635-1323.

DEEP RIVER

The Leather Man, Rattling Valley Road (Box 344),

06417. Professional. Frank Janoski specializes in leather articles; all are hand dyed and hand carved or hand tooled, and feature intricate painting and hand sewing. Prices range from 50¢ to $70.

Open October through June, daily 11 to 6; July through September, Monday through Thursday 11 to 8. **Directions:** Take Route 9 exit 4, then go left at the bottom of the ramp. After 1 mile, turn right onto Rattling Valley Road. At the bottom of the hill is a sign for the shop, which is ¼ mile ahead, on the right. (203) 526-9188.

EAST BROOKLYN

The Pine and Palette Studio (20 Ventura Drive, Danielson, 06239). Professional. Arlene and Bob Brown specialize in hand-crafted fireplace bellows of leather and wood with brass fittings, hand decorated with authentic patterns of the 1800s. Other items include theorem paintings and theorem Christmas ornaments in early American patterns, naturally stained and stenciled matchboxes in three sizes, and keg banks in hand-charred finishes. The Browns also refinish and re-leather antique bellows. Prices for bellows range from $4.95 to $54.95. The studio is located in the Brown home.

Open by appointment; please call. (203) 774-5058.

EAST KILLINGLY

Peep Toad Mill, Peep Toad Road (Box 108), 06243. Professional. Husband-and-wife team Richard and Sandra Farrell produce stoneware and porcelain pottery characterized by a simplicity of form and their unique glaze overlays that suggest landscape images. Items include dinnerware, bowls, mugs, and large slab planters. Also featured are two-dimensional tile paintings ranging in size from two by two feet to one hundred by two hundred feet, done on commission; stop by studio to see samples. Prices for pottery begin at $10. Peep Toad Mill has existed for nine years and operates out of a historic mill that dates from the eighteenth century. It also served as an axe and hoe shop, a saw and grist mill, a machine shop, and an early-nineteenth-century tannery. Special exhibitions include works in clay, metal, fiber, and glass. Visitors are welcome to stop by.

Open all year, by appointment or chance after 11 AM. **Directions:** Take Route 52 exit 93, then head east on Route 101 for 1.8 miles. Peep Toad Road is just off Route 101. (203) 774-8967.

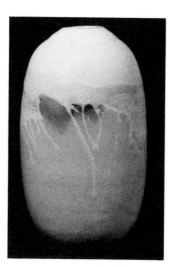

Porcelain vase by Sandra and Richard Farrell, Peep Toad Mill, East Killingly

EAST LYME

Waterford Weavers, 117B Boston Post Road, 06333.
Professional. Shop specializes in hand-woven tote bags,
wool and mohair stoles, baby blankets, wool afghans,
and yardage. Most goods are hand woven by shop
owner Marion Scannell.

Open all year, Tuesday through Saturday 10 to 5.
Directions: Take Interstate 95 exit 74, then head north
on Route 161 and turn left onto Boston Post Road
(Route 1). The shop is the second building on the right,
next to the Arco gasoline station. (203) 739-4001.

ESSEX

The Glass Basket, 69 Main Street, 06426. Professional
and amateur. Shop features hand-crafted miniatures,
especially birds and decoys; silver and 14-karat gold
designer jewelry; calicos and quilts; and pottery. Prices
range from $1.95 to $200. The shop is housed in a home
built in the 1700s, and is the exclusive outlet for many
of the crafts sold.

Open April through June, Monday through Saturday 10 to 5; July and August, Sunday through Thursday
10 to 5, Friday and Saturday to 9:30; September through
December, Monday through Saturday 10 to 5. **Directions:** Take Route 9 exit 3, and head east to Essex. The
shop is in the center of town, across from the Griswold
Inn. (203) 767-2350.

*Wool and mohair scarf by
Marion Scannell, Waterford
Weavers, East Lyme*

FAIRFIELD

**Roger Ludlowe Arts and Crafts Fair, Roger Ludlowe
School, Unquowa Road, 06430.** 2-day juried crafts fair,
sponsored by the Roger Ludlowe Parents Club and held
the Saturday and Sunday before Thanksgiving. Hours:
10 to 4:30. About 65 professional craftspeople exhibit
jewelry, pottery, silk-screened clothing, weaving, silk
and dried flowers, pillows, patchwork, small holiday
ornaments, shearling items, metal, and leather. Jewelry,
woodcarving, and puppetry are demonstrated. "One of
the things that give our show its special flavor is the
presence of *student* craftspeople, in addition to the professionals." Food available. Over 4,000 visitors annually. Admission charge. **Directions:** Take Interstate
95 exit 21, and follow Mill Plain Road north a short distance to the intersection with Unquowa Road. Turn
right onto Unquowa Road; the school is on the right.
(203) 259-6556.

Yarn Barn, 139 Tunxis Hill Road, 06430. Shop
features wooden toys and signs, wind chimes, dried and
silk flowers, and handmade holiday ornaments. Prices
range from 50¢ to $50.

**To get to Fairfield, take Inter-
state 95 exit 21 or 24.**

Painted totem by Douglas Eric Fuchs, The Elements Gallery, Greenwich

To get to Greenwich, take Interstate 95 exit 3.

Open all year, daily (except closed Wednesday and Sunday), 9:30 to 5. **Directions:** Take Interstate 95 exit 24 (Black Rock Turnpike) to Kings Highway, and follow Kings Highway to Villa Avenue. Take Villa Avenue to the junction with Tunxis Hill Road and turn onto Tunxis Hill Road; the shop is across from Bradlee's and Caldor's stores. (203) 334-1396.

FARMINGTON

Arts in Season Holiday Sale, Art Guild of Farmington, Church Street, 06032. A 10-day juried show, sponsored by the guild and held from the first weekend in December through the second. Hours: Monday through Friday 10 to 5, Saturday and Sunday to 6. Approximately 100 professional craftspeople and artists exhibit sculpture, pottery, quilts, wooden toys, paintings, prints, and photography. Admission charge on opening night. **Directions:** Take Interstate 84 exit 39 (Farmington), then head west on Route 4 about 1 mile. Turn left onto Route 10 (Main Street), and take the third left onto Church Street. (203) 677-6205.

GLASTONBURY

Craftsmanship in Wood, Inc., 27K Commerce Street, 06033. Professional and amateur. Shop features reproductions of Shaker and period furniture. Prices range from $10 to $5,000.

Open all year, Monday through Saturday 8 to 5. **Directions:** From Hartford take Route 2 south exit 8, and turn left at the end of the exit ramp. At the traffic light, turn right onto Oak Street. Commerce Street is the first left; the shop is on the corner. (203) 659-0767.

GREENWICH

The Elements Gallery, 14 Liberty Way, 06830. Professional. Selections include porcelain, woven goods, blown glass, and jewelry — all one-of-a-kind items produced by American craftspeople. Prices range from $10 to $500.

Open September through July, Tuesday through Saturday 10 to 5. **Directions:** Take Interstate 95 exit 3, go under the railroad bridge, then bear right onto Arch Street. Cross Greenwich Avenue, and turn left onto Mason Street, then left again onto Elm Street. Less than ½ block ahead on the right is a large parking lot; the shop is at the far end, in a brick building. (203) 661-0014.

Pottery by June, 22 Fairfield Road, 06830. Professional. Studio features the work of potter June Lund, who offers mugs, planters, pitchers, sugar-and-cream sets, and casseroles. Prices range from $5 to $200. The studio is located on an old country estate.

Open all year, by appointment only; please call. (203) 869-4397.

Why Not!, 71 Church Street, 06830. Professional and amateur. Shop offers functional pottery, "little people" soft sculpture, and original hand-knitted goods. Prices range from $5 to $300.

Open all year, Monday through Friday 9:30 to 5, Saturday to 1. **Directions:** From Interstate 95, take exit 3 to Railroad Avenue. Turn right onto Railroad Avenue, go to Mason Street, and follow Mason Street until it becomes Church Street. (203) 661-8383.

GUILFORD

To get to Guilford, take Interstate 95 exit 58 (Route 77).

Artisans Corner, 61 Whitfield Street, 06437. Professional and amateur. Shop selections include functional stoneware pottery, fountains, and aquariums; gold and silver jewelry; soft sculpture; children's toys; hand-carved tables; graphics such as paintings, brass rubbings, and lithographs; and silk-screened items. Prices range from $1.50 to $1,000.

Open all year, Monday through Saturday 10 to 5. **Directions:** Take Interstate 95 exit 58, turn south onto Route 77 (Church Street), then cross Route 1 and continue 1 block to Guilford green. Follow Route 77 to the right ½ block, and then turn left onto Whitfield Street. (203) 453-3122.

Guilford Handcraft Center, Route 77 (Box 221), 06437. Professional and amateur. The center offers works by nearly two hundred artisans. Selections include pottery, leather, metal, wood, glass, and fibers. Prices range from $1 to $100.

Open all year, Monday through Saturday 10 to 4, Sunday from 1. **Directions:** From Interstate 95 exit 58, turn north; the center is 100 yards ahead. (203) 453-5947.

Guilford Handcrafts Exposition and Sale, on the green. 3-day juried event sponsored by the Guilford Handcraft Center (Box 221, 06437) and held the third Thursday, Friday, and Saturday in July. Hours: noon to 9. About 100 professional craftspeople and students at the center exhibit and demonstrate pottery, leather, metal, woodwork, glass, and fiber crafts. Admission charge for adults; children under twelve free. 40,000 visitors annually. **Directions:** Take Interstate 95 exit 58 onto Route 77, and head south to the green. (203) 453-5947.

Nautical Treasures and Crafts, 124 Tuttle Point Road, 06437. Professional. Studio specializes in Ellen Graver's driftwood plaques, lobster-pot tables, and original driftwood lamps — all one of a kind. Prices range from $5 to $90.

Open all year, by appointment only; please call. (203) 453-9876.

HADDAM

Old Church Pottery and Gallery, Route 9A, 06438. Professional. Pottery/gallery specializes in high-fired stoneware, especially ring bottles and flower or reed holders thrown with three or more colored clays together. Prices range from $4.50 to $55. The pottery/gallery is in a former Baptist church built in 1833.

Open all year, Monday through Saturday 10 to 5:30, Sunday from 11. **Directions:** From Hartford, take Route 9 south exit 10, then head south on Route 9A to the shop (about 5 miles). (203) 345-4124.

HAMDEN

The Craft Fair, 2510 Whitney Avenue, 06518. Professional and amateur. Selections include handmade stuffed dolls, quilts, wooden toys, stained glass, ceramic dinnerware and canister sets, calligraphy, macramé, and enamel jewelry. Prices range from $2 to $50. Items featured are the works of thirty-five craftspeople.

Open September through December, Monday through Saturday 10 to 5; January through August, Tuesday through Saturday 11 to 4. **Directions:** Take Interstate 91 exit 10 (Route 40 connector). At the end of the exit ramp, turn left onto Whitney Avenue; the store is about 6 blocks ahead, on the right. (203) 288-5507.

E. Gloria Hoffenberg's, 39 Carroll Road, 06517. Professional. Hoffenberg specializes in wall hangings and pillows done in creative stitchery, and also carries original patchwork and quilted goods. Prices range from $20 to $650.

Open all year, by appointment only; please call. (203) 288-2198 evenings.

Yankee Woodcraft, 3569 Whitney Avenue, 06518. Professional. Shop specializes in oval frames and mirrors hand crafted from eastern white pine, plus clocks, corner shelves, and hardwood cutting boards. Shop owners Paul and Jim Dringoli emphasize "quality finish and elegance in design." Prices range from $3 to $39.

Open all year, daily 5 PM to 8 PM, but appointment is suggested. **Directions:** The shop is on Route 10. (203) 248-0281.

Wine decanter, Old Church Pottery and Gallery, Haddam

To get to Hamden, take Interstate 91 exit 10 onto the Route 40 connector. Or, take Interstate 84 exit 26 onto Route 70 south to Cheshire; then turn right and follow Route 10.

HARTFORD

Hartford Christmas Crafts Expos I and II, Hartford Civic Center. A pair of 3-day juried crafts shows, sponsored by American Crafts Expositions, Inc. (Box 368,

Canton, 06019) and held the first and second weekends in December. Hours: Friday noon to 9, Saturday 10 to 9, Sunday 10 to 8. Approximately 250 professional craftspeople from throughout the United States are in attendance. Continuous crafts demonstrations. Refreshments available. 25,000 visitors annually. Admission charge for adults; children under ten free if accompanied by parents. **Directions:** Take Interstate 84 exit for Ann Street or High Street, and follow signs to the civic center. (203) 693-6311.

LAKESIDE

Hilcraft, Hickory Hill Road, 06758. Professional. Shop specializes in pewter manufactured by a father-and-son team. Offerings include baby dishes and spoons, candle holders, sugar-and-cream sets, and jewelry. Custom orders accepted. Prices range from $5 to $100.

Open all year, Monday through Friday afternoons, and by appointment; please call ahead. (203) 567-9860.

LITCHFIELD

Annual Litchfield Arts and Crafts Show, Route 202. A 2-day juried show, sponsored by the Litchfield Auxiliary of the Child and Family Services of Northwest Connecticut (564 Prospect Street, Torrington, 06790) and held during Columbus Day weekend. Hours: 11 to 5. About 60 professional and amateur artisans offer works in many areas of arts and crafts. Quilting, weaving, blacksmithing, pottery, woodworking, pewter, and soft sculpture are demonstrated continuously. Refreshments available. 6,000 visitors annually. Admission charge. (203) 567-0634.

Cobble Court Creative Arts, Cobble Court, 06759. Professional. Selections include forged iron, wind chimes, quilting, prints, jewelry, pillows, stained glass, and leather. Prices range from $5 to $200. All goods sold are the work of Connecticut craftspeople.

Open all year, Monday through Saturday 10 to 5; plus open June through October, Sunday 11 to 4. **Directions:** The shop is in the center of town, in an enclosed cobble court. (203) 567-8992.

To get to Litchfield, take Route 8 exit 38, then head northwest on Route 254 to town.

MANCHESTER

Walt Scadden, Blacksmith, 22 Warren Street, 06040. Professional. Shop specializes in hand-forged colonial-style hardware. Prices range from $1 to $800.

Open September through May, Monday through Saturday 8:30 to 4:30; June through August, Monday through Friday 8:30 to 4:30, Saturday to noon; but please call ahead. **Directions:** Take Interstate 84 to the

23

Main Street (Route 83) exit in Manchester. Then follow South Main Street for .1 mile, and turn right onto Warren Street. The shop is at the end of the street, on the left. (203) 646-8363.

MERIDEN

Meriden "Meet the Artists and Artisans" Show, Meriden Square shopping center. 4-day juried arts and crafts show sponsored by Denise Morris Curt (41 Green Street, Milford, 06460) and held the third weekend in October. Hours: Thursday through Saturday 10 to 9:30, Sunday noon to 5. This indoor event features one hundred exhibitors. Admission free. **Directions:** Take Interstate 91 exit 6 (Lewis Avenue) to Route 66. Head west on Route 66 toward Meriden. (203) 874-5672.

MIDDLETOWN

To get to Middletown, take Interstate 91 exit 18 onto Route 66. Or, take Interstate 91 exit 22 onto Route 9.

Middletown Chapter of Hadassah Annual Craft Fair, Riverview Center Parking Arcade, Court Street. 1-day crafts event, sponsored by the Middletown Chapter of Hadassah and held in September. Hours: 10 to 5. Approximately 200 professional and amateur craftspeople display scrimshaw, lapidary, gold and silver jewelry, leather, sand terrariums, batik, doll-house miniatures, woodworking, and holiday ornaments. The making of sand terrariums is demonstrated. Food available. 10,000 visitors annually. Admission free. **Directions:** Take Interstate 91 exit 18 (Route 66). Follow Route 66 east about 10 miles, then turn right onto Main Street. Court Street is the first left. (203) 347-7765.

Wesleyan Potters Annual Exhibit and Sale, Wesleyan Potters Craft Center, 350 South Main Street, 06457. A 16-day juried event, sponsored by Wesleyan Potters and beginning the Saturday after Thanksgiving. Hours: daily 10 to 8. About 280 professionals and amateurs exhibit crafts ranging from functional and decorative stoneware and porcelain to textiles, metal, glass, and jewelry. The exhibit/sale is held in a converted weaving mill. Over 5,000 visitors annually. **Directions:** From Route 9 in Middletown, take the exit for Route 17 south (New Haven). At the end of the exit, go ¾ of the way around the traffic circle, onto South Main Street. The pottery headquarters is on the left, after the second traffic light. (203) 347-5925.

MILFORD

To get to Milford, take Interstate 95 exit 37 or 39A. Or, follow Route 8 south to Route 108; then take Route 108 to Route 1, and head east on Route 1 (Boston Post Road) about 5 miles.

Dey's Leather Shack, 19 River Street, 06460. Professional. Shop specializes in stamped, elaborately tooled, and stained belts made on the premises. Also carries boots, handbags, wallets, and watch bands.

Open all year, Monday through Saturday 10 to 5:30,

plus open Thursday to 8:30. **Directions:** Heading south on Interstate 95, take exit 39A. At Howard Johnson's and the fork, bear left onto Cherry Street. Follow Cherry Street to the green; River Street is just ahead. The shop is just beyond the railroad underpass, on the left. (203) 878-7206.

Milford Green "Meet the Artists and Artisans" Show. 2-day juried crafts show, sponsored by Denise Morris Curt (41 Green Street, 06460) and held during Memorial Day weekend. Hours: Saturday and Sunday 10 to 5, rain or shine. Almost 200 exhibitors are in attendance. Admission free. **Directions:** The green is 1 block north of the harbor, and is just south of Route 1. (203) 874-5672.

MOODUS

Down on the Farm, Ltd., Banner Road, 06469. Professional. The center features contemporary American crafts made by more than 350 artisans. Selections include pottery, art glass, batik, leather, and turned wood. Pieces cost $1 to $500 and up. Down on the Farm is in a renovated chicken coop on a working poultry farm, with studios on the premises.

Open April through mid-January, Tuesday through Sunday (plus open Monday holidays) 11 to 5. **Directions:** Take Route 2 exit 16, and turn right at the end of the exit, onto Route 149S. At the second blinking light (about 7 miles ahead), turn right and, after .8 mile, take the first left. Go up the hill to the center, which is on the right, opposite a golf course. (203) 873-9905.

MYSTIC

Olde Mistick Village Art and Handcrafts Show. 2-day juried show, sponsored by Denise Morris Curt (41 Green Street, Milford, 06460) and held the first weekend in September. Hours: 10 to 6. About 90 craftspeople and artists exhibit handcrafts, paintings, sculpture and graphics. Admission free. **Directions:** Take Interstate 95 exit 90 onto Route 27. (203) 874-5672.

NEW CANAAN

Silvermine Guild of Artists, Inc., 1037 Silvermine Road, 06840. Professional. Selections include silver, brass, and enamel jewelry; pottery; blown glass; and hand-woven wall hangings and clothing. Prices range from $5 to $1,000. The guild holds a Christmas Crafts Exhibition in the Silvermine Guild Gallery each year from the Saturday before Thanksgiving through December 24, with one hundred exhibitors displaying crafts in many media, plus special holiday creations.

Admission to Christmas exhibition is free.

Shop open all year, Tuesday through Sunday 12:30 to 5. (Christmas Crafts Exhibition days and hours also conform to this schedule.) **Directions:** Take Interstate 95 exit 15, and turn right at the end of the ramp (at the traffic light). At the second traffic light, turn right again, then right again at the next traffic light, onto Silvermine Avenue. Follow Silvermine Avenue 1½ miles, to a stop sign. Then turn left onto Silvermine Road. (203) 966-5617.

NEW FAIRFIELD

Jean Mann, Route 39 (RFD 1, Box 27), 06810. Professional. Mann specializes in one-of-a-kind wheel-thrown, hand-carved, high-fired porcelain, in Chinese styles and copper-red glazes. Prices begin at $50.

Open by appointment only; please call. (203) 746-4969.

NEW HAVEN

To get to the New Haven shops, take Interstate 91 exit for downtown New Haven.

Derek Simpson, Goldsmith, 46 High Street, 06511. Professional. Shop specializes in jewelry, mainly gold, set with precious and semiprecious stones in contemporary styles. All pieces are created on the premises by Derek Simpson and his associates.

Open all year, Monday through Friday 10 to 5:30, Saturday to 5; closed Monday in summer. **Directions:** Take Interstate 91 downtown New Haven exit, then turn right at the end of the ramp, onto York Street. Take the first right, onto George Street, then turn left onto High Street. The shop is in the Yale Center for British Art, on the first floor. (203) 787-2498.

Peter Indorf, Fine Jewelers and Designers, 1177 Chapel Street, 06511. Professional. Indorf specializes in gold and silver handmade jewelry, incorporating diamonds, pearls, and colored stones into many pieces. Custom orders accepted. Prices range from $25 to $2,000. Featured are "simple, classic, tailored designs."

Open all year, Tuesday through Saturday 11 to 5. **Directions:** Take Interstate 91 exit for Route 34, and follow to downtown New Haven. Turn right onto York Street; then, at the third traffic light, turn left onto Chapel Street. Go 1 block, to the junction with Park Street; the shop is on the corner, on the right. (203) 776-4833.

NEW MILFORD

To get to New Milford, take Interstate 84 exit 7 in Danbury, and head north on Route 7.

Crossways Studio, Long Mountain Road, 06776. Professional. Studio sells batik pillows and quilts, wall hangings, and hand-painted ceramic lamp bases. Custom orders accepted. Prices range from $7 to $150.

Open all year, Monday through Saturday 10 to 4. **Directions:** Take Route 7 to Gaylordsville, and turn onto Long Mountain Road. (203) 354-7170.

Voltaire's — the Shop and Gallery, Route 7, 06776. Professional. Selections include weaving, leather, jewelry, ceramics, glass, wood, and wrought iron. Prices range from $7.50 to $500. Shop features the works of over fifty American craftspeople.

Open all year, Monday through Saturday 10 to 5. **Directions:** The shop/gallery is 2½ miles north of the town's traffic circle at the junction of routes 7 and 37. (203) 354-4200.

Sculpture, Voltaire's, New Milford

NEW PRESTON

Wolff Pottery, Route 202, Woodville, 06777. Professional. Potter Guy Wolff specializes in a complete line of American and English stoneware and horticultural earthenware. Prices range from $3 to $60.

Open weekends 11 to 5; other times, by appointment. **Directions:** The shop is about 8 miles southwest of Litchfield, and 12 miles northeast of New Milford; Woodville is a section of New Preston. (203) 868-2858.

NEWTOWN

a Weaver and a Potter, 33 Main Street, 06470. Professional. Shop features hand-woven place mats, handbags, scarves, shawls, and throws; also sells stoneware, serving bowls, cooking ware, and lamps. Pieces cost $4 to $30 and up.

Open all year, Tuesday through Saturday 10 to 5. **Directions:** Take Interstate 84 exit 9 or 10 to Route 25 (Main Street). The shop is in the center of town. (203) 426-4155.

NIANTIC

A Touch of Glass, 48 Pennsylvania Avenue, 06357. Professional. Shop specializes in stained-glass windows, plus lamp shades, mirrors, clocks, and boxes created by Anthony Artino. Items cost $5 to $450 and up. "Quality work and unique design are the two Artino trademarks."

Open all year, Saturday 10 to 4; plus open other times by appointment. **Directions:** Take Interstate 95 exit 72, and head south to Route 156. Follow Route 156 to the center of town, then turn left onto Pennsylvania Avenue and go 1 block. (203) 739-5544.

NORTH HAVEN

Edwin Haag, Woodcraft, 11 Ansonia Drive, 06473.
Professional. Haag creates wood products in oak, cherry, walnut, and some pine. All pieces are functional, yet simply designed. Prices range from $2.50 to $250.

Open all year, Monday through Saturday by appointment only; please call. (203) 239-0719.

NORWALK

Artists' Market, Inc., 319 Main Avenue, 06851. Professional. Shop sells blown glass, paperweights, pottery, limited-edition prints, vases, and footstools made to resemble feet wearing sneakers or ski boots. Prices range from $10 to $500. "We are very selective and purchase only what we love."

Open all year, Tuesday through Saturday 10 to 5. **Directions:** Take the Merritt Parkway to exit 39, and then head south ½ mile. The shop is on the right. (203) 846-2550.

NORWICH

Edgerton's Handcrafts, 210 West Town Street, 06360.
Professional. Kate Edgerton offers yarns and handwoven fabrics. Prices range from $5 to $150. The shop is located in a private home built in 1660.

Open all year, most any time. **Directions:** Take Interstate 95 (which is also the Connecticut Turnpike and becomes Route 52) to exit 82 in Norwich. The shop is just west of the exit. (203) 889-5990.

OLD LYME

Pfeiffer Studio, 132 Whippoorwill Road, 06371. Professional. Studio specializes in cloisonné jewelry in traditional designs, and silver and vermeil settings. Also carries rosewood and pewter boxes, silver castings, and sculptured jewelry of cast silver. Custom orders accepted. Pieces cost $10 to $100 and up.

Open by appointment only; please call. (203) 434-5621.

To get to Old Saybrook, take Interstate 95 exit 65, 66, 67, or 68. Or, take Route 9 exit 2, then follow Route 154 south.

OLD SAYBROOK

The Anderson-Williams House, 47 Mohican Road, Cornfield Point, 06475. Professional. Hank Williams does chair seating such as cane, fiber, splint, and Shaker taping. His specialty is natural rush in cat-o'-nine-tails. Pieces cost $8 to $25 and up. Seat-weaving demonstrations are given.

Open September through June, Monday through

Saturday 8 to 3; July through August, Monday through Saturday 8 to noon; but best to call ahead. **Directions:** From Route 9, take exit 2 and turn right onto Route 154. At the third traffic light (in Saybrook), turn left onto Main Street (still Route 154). Continue to the second traffic light, and turn right onto Maple Avenue; follow it to the stop sign and go through the intersection (where the route becomes Town Beach Road). At the third stop sign on Town Beach Road, turn left onto Mohican Road; look for a brown two-story house at the crest of the hill, on the right. (203) 388-2587.

Critters by Otis, 75 Hartford Avenue, 06475. Professional and amateur. Theodore Otis Soule creates "critters" in clay, metal, and wood, mostly from objects he finds — farm equipment, spades, shovels, bicycle parts, pulleys, springs, pipe fittings, and rakes. "Critters" range in size from six inches to six feet; all are animated by springs or motors with lights for control panels, hearts, noses, and eyes. Prices range from $5 to $500.

Open all year, by appointment; please call. (203) 388-3894.

Coffeepot with decorative painting by Jean Hansen, The Tinker's Painter, Old Saybrook

The Sampler, 1712 Boston Post Road (Box 53), 06480. Shop features finished quilts from crib- to king-sized, plus quilted pillows and wall hangings. Prices range from $25 to $500.

Open all year, Monday through Saturday 10 to 5. **Directions:** Take Interstate 95 exit 66, then follow Route 166 south to Route 1 (Boston Post Road). Turn left onto Route 1; the shop is just ahead, on the left. (203) 399-7477.

The Tinker's Painter, Chalker Village Complex, 1550 Boston Post Road, 06475. Professional and amateur. Shop features a large display of decorative painting by owner Jean S. Hansen. The display reflects a contemporary view of the history of decorative painting techniques, from oils to acrylics and water colors. Hansen's emphasis is on the presentation of decorative art techniques as forms of folk art. Prices begin at $5.

Open all year, Monday through Saturday 9 to 5. **Directions:** Take Interstate 95 east exit 66, then turn right onto Route 166. Follow Route 166 to the first traffic light, and turn left onto Route 1; the complex is about ¼ mile ahead. Or, heading west on Interstate 95, take exit 66 and turn left onto Route 166. (203) 399-5217.

QUINEBAUG

Grandmother's Toys, Walker Road (Box 39, Fabyan, 06245). Studio owner Betty Winslow specializes in soft dolls. Prices range from $1 to $100.

Open all year, by chance or appointment. **Directions:** Take Interstate 86 exit 105 to Route 190. Follow Route 190 northeast to Route 197, then follow Route

197 northeast, through Fabyan, to Quinebaug. Walker Street is between routes 197 and 131. (203) 935-9127.

RIVERTON

Contemporary Crafts Gallery, Route 20 (Box 109), 06065. Professional. Gallery features the work of designer-pewterer James R. Gagnon, who makes flatware and hollowware. Also carries other original works such as puppets, blown-glass goblets, fiber, ceramics, paintings, and other graphics. Prices range from $5 to $5,000. The gallery "blends fine craft with fine art."

Open all year (except closed between Christmas and New Year's days), Tuesday through Saturday 11 to 5, Sunday noon to 4. **Directions:** Take Route 8 north to Winsted (where the route ends), then follow Route 20 north to Riverton. (203) 379-2964.

SALISBURY

Undermountain Weavers, Ltd., Undermountain Road, 06068. Professional. Shop specializes in hand-woven tweeds and cashmeres with an emphasis on scarves, ties, and other clothing. Prices range from $15 to $350.

Usually open most days, but please call. **Directions:** From Hartford or Route 8 (Winsted), head west on Route 44 to Route 41. Then head north on Route 41 about 4½ miles beyond the center of Salisbury. (203) 435-2321.

Nikky clown by Betty Winslow, Grandmother's Toys, Quinebaug

SOMERSVILLE

Somersville Crafts Gallery, 49 Maple Street, 06072. Professional. Selections include glass, tinware, enamel on copper, toys, lithographs, weaving, jewelry, wall hangings, dried-flower arrangements, bookbinding, and chair caning. Prices range from $5 to $2,000.

Open March through December, Tuesday through Saturday 10 to 5, Sunday from noon; January and February, Wednesday through Saturday 10 to 5, Sunday from noon; closed major holidays. **Directions:** From Interstate 91 near Enfield, head east on Route 190 to Somersville, then turn south onto Maple Street. The gallery is 300 yards ahead, in a building next to the waterfall. (203) 749-3684.

SOUTHBURY

Yobo Enterprises, 832 Old Waterbury Road, 06488. Professional and amateur. Shop owner Julie Bowers specializes in patchwork quilts and pillows. Prices range from $5 to $125.

Open all year, by appointment. (203) 264-9622.

STAMFORD

Design Studio, 885 High Ridge Road, 06905. Professional. David Goldfarb offers his own designs in sterling silver and gold jewelry. Goldfarb will also work with a customer's idea, from design through execution. Repair work done. Prices range from $8 to $800.

Open all year, Tuesday through Saturday 10 to 5:30. **Directions:** Take the Merritt Parkway exit 35 to High Ridge Road. (203) 322-8828.

Gingham Dog and Calico Cat, 44 Sixth Street, Ridgeway Shopping Center, 06905. Professional and amateur. Selections include hand-crafted toys, baby things, household accessories, quilts, and soft sculpture. Prices range from $1 to $300.

Open all year, Monday through Saturday 10 to 5. **Directions:** Take Merritt Parkway exit 35 south to Ridgeway Shopping Center. (203) 327-5740.

The Quest for Handcrafts, 2299 Summer Street, 06905. Professional. Shop features contemporary crafts from thirty states. Selections include pottery, jewelry, weaving, batik, glass, leather, and wood. Prices range from $5 to $500.

Open all year, Monday through Saturday 10 to 5:30, plus Thursday to 9; also open between Thanksgiving and Christmas, Monday through Friday to 9; plus month of December, Sunday 11 to 5:30. **Directions:** Take Interstate 95 exit 7 to Atlantic Street. Go 1½ miles north on Atlantic Street (Atlantic Street becomes Bedford Street, which the shop also faces) to the Ridgeway Shopping Center. The shop is within the Forty Boutiques Mall section of the center. (203) 324-2660.

To get to Stamford, take the Merritt Parkway exit 35. Or, take Interstate 95 exit 7.

STORRS

Jan Scottron, 576 Browns Road, 06268. Professional. Scottron features her own hand-bound books, as well as pads, telephone-book covers, clipboards, and date books. Repair work done. Prices range from $2 to $20.

Open by appointment only. (203) 423-6614.

TRUMBULL

Peter M. Petrochko, Designer and Craftsman, 40 McGuire Road, 06611. Professional. In his home studio-shop, Petrochko creates wooden canister sets, bowls, vases, furniture, clocks, and jewelry boxes. Prices range from $5 to $75. Petrochko uses his architectural and fine arts backgrounds to produce "unique, functional crafts."

Open all year, Monday through Saturday 10 to 6. **Directions:** From Norwalk, take Route 15 north to exit 50; at the end of the exit ramp, turn right and go 1 mile

Copper lantern by Serge Miller, Washington Copper Works, Washington

on White Plains Road to Trumbull center. Then turn right onto Daniels Farm Road, drive 3 miles north to a stop sign, and then, at the fork, bear right onto McGuire Road. Petrochko's studio is just ahead, in a large house with redwood trim. (203) 268-8462.

WASHINGTON

The Washington Copper Works, South Street, 06793. Professional. Shop specializes in copper lighting fixtures for both indoors and out, designed and created by shop owner Serge Miller. Prices range from $8 to $1,000. "Although the fixtures are made much the way they were two centuries ago, they are my designs."

Open all year, Monday through Friday 9:30 to 6; call for Saturday and Sunday open hours. **Directions:** Take Interstate 84 exit 15 (Southbury) and head north on routes 6 and 67 to Route 47. Turn left onto Route 47, go 7½ miles, and then turn left onto South Street. The shop is ½ mile ahead, on the right (opposite the shop driveway are a blue and a silver mailbox). (203) 868-7527 weekdays, 868-7637 weekends.

WATERFORD

Howmar Crafts, 151 Great Neck Road, 06385. Professional. Shop specializes in hand-carved wall plaques, mirrors, and anchors, each with attached hand-carved wood figures of birds, fish, or other animals. Prices range from $6 to $35.

Open all year, Monday through Thursday 9 to 7. **Directions:** Take Interstate 95 exit 75 to Route 1, then follow Route 1 south to Route 156. Head west on Route 156 to Route 213, then south on Route 213. (203) 442-2986.

WESTPORT

Gilbertie Herb Gardens, Sylvan Avenue, 06880. Professional and amateur. Shop specializes in hand-fashioned herbal wreaths and other herbal decorations. Prices range from $10 to $50.

Open October through December, Monday through Saturday 8:30 to 5:30. **Directions:** Take Interstate 95 exit 17, then go 1 mile north to the shop. (203) 227-4175.

WEST STAFFORD

Creativ Endeavors, Route 190 (442 West Stafford Road, Stafford Springs, 06076). Professional. Shop features the work of members of the Glass Artisans Guild, a group of craftspeople who create unique stained-glass furnishings such as full-sized grandmother clocks, and tables. Also sells hand-dipped candles, calligraphy, functional pottery, and leather. Items cost $5 to $1,000 and up. The shop is housed in the historic Bradway Machine Works building.

Open all year, Tuesday through Sunday noon to 6. **Directions:** Take Interstate 91 exit 74E onto Route 190. Head east on Route 190 (West Stafford Road) about 13 miles. (203) 684-4894.

WETHERSFIELD

The Second Floor Store, 271 Main Street, 06109. Professional and amateur. Selections include stained glass, pottery, wood, painted eggs, pocketbooks, pillows, place mats, and napkins. Items cost $1 to $20 and up.

Open all year (except closed last two weeks in July), Tuesday through Saturday 10 to 5; plus open November and December, Sunday 1 to 5. (203) 563-5727.

Toys in the Attic, 271 Main Street, 06109. Professional and amateur. Selections include doll houses hand crafted by Gary McLeod, both in kit form and assembled. Also carries hand-crafted miniature furniture, dolls, pillows, and accessories by Jeanne McLeod.

Open all year, Tuesday through Saturday 10 to 5; plus open October through December, Sunday 1 to 5. (203) 563-2224.

To get to Wethersfield, take Interstate 91 exit 26 (Marsh Street) and follow signs to "Historic District." Turn right at Main Street; the shops are across the street from a large church.

WINDHAM CENTER

Laura Knott Twine — Weaving, Spinning, and Looms, Route 14 (Box 368), 06280. Twine offers a wide variety of woven creations, including clothing, rugs, curtains, table cloths, and contemporary wall hangings. Prices range from $15 to $400.

Open all year, Monday through Saturday 10 to 5. (203) 423-7355.

Country Classics from Unique Pinecone Creations, 19 Oakwood Drive, 06280. Professional. Linda-Jo Stevens crafts pine-cone wreaths, ducks, owls, and baskets; also herbal wreaths and arrangements and dried flowers. Prices range from $3 to $60.

Open all year, by chance or appointment. **Directions:** Take Route 14 about 1¼ miles east of the town green, to Oakwood Drive; turn right onto Oakwood Drive. (203) 456-1273.

To get to Windham Center, take Route 2 exit 13, then follow Route 66 northeast to Route 6. Take Route 6 east to Willimantic, then Route 14 east to Windham Center.

WINSTED

Folkcraft Instruments, 99 High Street (Box 807), 06098. Professional. Shop owners David and Susan Marks feature hand-crafted folk instruments in finished form and in kits — Appalachian mountain dulcimers, hammered dulcimers, banjos, mandolins, folk harps, and psalteries. Prices range from $20 to $395.

Open all year, Tuesday through Friday 10 to 5, Saturday and evenings by appointment. **Directions:** Take Route 8 north to Winsted or, from Hartford, take Route 44 west. At the traffic light after the movie theater, turn right; the shop is on the left, at the corner of High and Wheeler streets, opposite Connecticut Bank and Trust. (203) 379-7685.

To get to Wolcott, take Interstate 84 exit 24, then follow Route 69 north.

WOLCOTT

Dovic Dolls, 52 Clinton Hill Road, 06716. Professional. Shop owner-craftsperson Dorothy Kohlberg specializes in rag dolls, from ten inches to five feet tall, in styles from old fashioned to modern. The most popular models are the recently designed Penny Pig and Flapper Flo. Custom orders accepted. Prices range from $10 to $85.

Open all year, by appointment only; please call. (203) 879-0945.

One of a Kind Creations, by Avak, 95 Allentown Road, 06716. Professional. Shop features rare and exotic butterflies enhancing clocks, lamps, coffee tables, and other items crafted by George Avak.

Open all year, by appointment. (203) 879-1513.

To get to Woodbury, take Interstate 84 exit 15, then follow routes 6 and 67 north.

WOODBURY

M.G. Martin, 580 Upper Grassy Hill Road, 06798. Professional. Martin specializes in ceramic tiles and outdoor planters. Also does mosaics, papier mâché, and batik. Prices range from $10 to $200.

Open all year, by appointment. (203) 263-3908.

Woodbury Pewterers, 860 Main Street South, 06798. Professional. Selections include handmade pewter bowls, candlesticks, coffee pots, mugs, tankards, and teapots. Many pieces are reproductions from the Henry Ford Museum Collection. Prices begin at $4.50.

Open May through December, Monday through Saturday 9 to 5; January through April, Monday through Friday 9 to 5. **Directions:** Take Interstate 84 exit 15, and go 3 miles north on Route 6; the shop is in a small, red-brick building on the left, just south of the center of town. (203) 263-2668.

Wood Reserve, 828 Main Street South, 06798. Professional. Shop specializes in redwood-burl furniture and hand-crafted accessories. Selections include glass-top tables, using bases made from naturally shaped roots and burls; all-wood tables in free-form polished wood; bars, ottomans, and chairs. Prices begin at $10.

Open April through December, Wednesday through Sunday 11 to 5. **Directions:** Take Interstate 84 exit 15, and head north on Route 6. The shop is on the left, just beyond Woodbury Pewterers. (203) 263-3786.

A *YANKEE* GUIDEBOOK

HANDCRAFT CENTERS OF NEW ENGLAND

II.
Maine

L
ike the other New England states, Maine has its share of crafts shops well off the beaten thruway. But here, perhaps more easily than in any of the other six states, you'll also find a recognizable trail of crafts centers: nearly every town along Route 1 boasts at least one crafts shop, studio, or fair. Since this popular tourist route roughly parallels the Maine coastline, a trip linking a number of crafts outlets can not only delight the crafts enthusiast but can also entice the reluctant shopper in the family to come along for a beautiful ride. Best of all, most of the shops throughout the state are open right up until Christmas, and many of them all year long; if you're too busy sunning and sailing to do much summertime shopping, Aunt Gertrude's Christmas present could be the perfect excuse to return to the crafts trails of Maine in December.

Sculptured bird, The Andersen Studio, East Boothbay

ABBOT VILLAGE

Crow Hill Pottery (RFD 1), 04406. Professional. Shop specializes in functional stoneware pottery that features unusual, bright glazes. Prices range from $1.50 to $150.

Open mid-June to Labor Day, daily 10:30 to 5. **Directions:** From Interstate 95, take Route 7 north to Route 23. Follow Route 23 north to junction with routes 6, 15, and 16; then head west to town, about 5 miles past Guilford and 30 miles south of Moosehead Lake. The shop is across from Titcomb's General Store. (207) 876-2657.

ALBION

Mason Studio, China Road, 04910. Professional. Studio specializes in twin-, double-, and queen-sized quilts; sweaters knitted from Maine wool; and patchwork pocketbooks, place mats, pot holders, and clothing. Prices range from 30¢ to $75. All work is done by designer-owner Andrea Mason in her home studio.

Open October through December 24, daily; January through September, by appointment only — please call first. **Directions:** From Interstate 95 in Augusta, head northeast on routes 9 and 202 to China. The studio is about 3½ miles beyond China. (207) 437-4163.

Vase by Bruce Kornbluth, Chosen Works, Bangor

ALFRED

Greenhouse Gallery, Cindy Taylor Clark, Route 202 (Box 6), 04002. Professional. Gallery features colonial tinware, hand crafted with folk-art designs; quilts; and water colors. Prices range from $3 to $300. The gallery makes an effort to handle "only selected crafts of area artisans who are trying to keep traditional crafts alive."

Open all year, Wednesday through Saturday 10 to 5. **Directions:** Take Interstate 95 exit 4, then head west on Route 111 for 10 miles. At the intersection with routes 4 and 202, turn right onto Route 202. The gallery is in the fifth house on the left, behind Chem-Clean Furniture Restoration. (207) 324-7903.

AUBURN

Maple Hill Pottery Craft Gallery, 158 Court Street, 04210. Professional. Pottery is made by shop owner Nancy Lee. Other selections include 14-karat gold and sterling silver jewelry, and hand-woven rugs, clothing, and baskets. Prices range from under $5 to $50. Maple Hill carries one-of-a-kind products, and craftspeople from all over the United States are represented.

Open all year, Monday through Thursday 10 to 8, Friday and Saturday to 9:30. **Directions:** Heading south on Interstate 95, take exit 12, and go left at the end of the ramp. Then go 4½ miles, and take a right onto Court Street. (207) 783-9283.

BANGOR

To get to Bangor, take Interstate 95 to any Bangor exit.

Chosen Works, 35 Central Street, 04401. Professional. Selections include pottery, handmade furniture, knitted and crocheted goods, stained glass, silk-screened graphics, lithographs, quilts, leather work, and jewelry. Items cost $4 to $1,000 and up. "Individuals perform as a group here, yet we do not lose our individuality."

Open all year, Monday through Saturday 10 to 5:30. **Directions:** The shop is downtown. (207) 947-3418.

Once Upon an Island, 14 Broad Street (50 Meadowbrook Road), 04401. Professional and amateur. Selections include appliquéd clothing, quilts, and accessories. Also carries porcelain and other pottery, paintings, and jewelry. Prices range from $10 to $2,500.

Open all year, Monday through Saturday 10 to 5. **Directions:** The shop is in the center of town, facing the fountain. (207) 945-6631.

BAR HARBOR

To get to Bar Harbor, follow routes 1 and 3 east until they fork, just beyond Ellsworth. Then follow Route 3 south to Bar Harbor.

Caleb's Sunrise, 115 Main Street, 04609. Professional. Selections include craft works from the state of Maine, in all media. The shop offers a wide variety of owner Leah Rae Donahue's one-of-a-kind leather handbag designs. Prices range from $3 to $400.

Open June through September, daily 9 AM to 11 PM. **Directions:** The shop is in the center of town. (207) 288-3102.

Great Lakes Dulcimers, 118 Ledgelawn Street, 04609. Professional. Shop specializes in Edward and Anne Damm's handmade dulcimers, Finnish kanteles, children's harps, lyres, Irish harps, bodhrans, and steel drums. Prices range from $3 to $450. All instruments are "sturdy, well crafted, and easy to learn to play."

Open all year, by appointment only. (207) 288-5653.

Island Craft Cooperative, Gull Building, Main Street, 04609. Professional. The cooperative features quilts, silk-screened textiles, batik wall hangings and sculptures, hand-woven clothing, fine furniture, and stoneware lamps and other pottery. Prices range from $5 to $3,000. "We are a collective of thirteen professional Mount Desert Island craftspeople."

Open Memorial Day through mid-October, daily 10 to 10. **Directions:** The shop is located in the center of town. (207) 288-4214.

BATH

Heritage Days Craft Fair, City Park, Washington Street. 2-day juried crafts fair, sponsored by Yankee Artisan (178 Front Street, 04530) and Bath Heritage Days Committee and held during Fourth of July week. Hours: 10 to 5. About 35 professional and amateur craftspeople exhibit woodcarvings, clay, fiber, leather, lapidary and other jewelry, and furniture. Entertainment. Admission free. **Directions:** City Park is less than ½ mile from Route 1. (207) 443-2787.

Yankee Artisan, 178 Front Street, 04530. Professional and amateur. Selections include stoneware animal-shaped baking dishes; sweaters, hats, socks, and mittens knitted from Maine wool; pottery; toys; woodcarvings; weaving; tiles; and rope creations. Prices range from 50¢ to $250. Craftspeople represented here must be permanent residents of Maine. All new crafts are juried to maintain high quality.

Open all year, Monday through Saturday 9 to 5. **Directions:** From Route 1, turn left onto Vine Street, and go to the top of the hill. Then turn left onto Front Street, the main street in town. (207) 443-6215.

To get to Bath, take Route 1 (Leeman Highway) to the center of town.

BLUE HILL

Rackliffe Pottery, Ellsworth Road, 04614. Professional. The Rackliffe family specializes in wheel-thrown pottery of native clay. Complete dinner sets are available, as well as jelly sets, vases, and casseroles. Prices range from $2 to $95. Pottery is created in simple shapes. The Rackliffes' specialty is Blue Hill blue glaze.

Open all year, Monday through Saturday 8 to 4; plus July and August, Sunday noon to 4. **Directions:** The shop is on Route 172, northeast of town. (207) 374-2297.

To get to Blue Hill, take Route 1 east, through Bucksport, to Route 15. Then take Route 15 south 14 miles to Blue Hill.

Rowantrees Pottery, 04614. Professional and amateur. Selections include traditional dinnerware, beverage and condiment servers, casseroles, pitchers, bean pots, platters, and bowls. Prices range from $4.50 to $60. All items are hand modeled or wheel thrown and use local clays and minerals. This village organization was originally established in 1934 to keep artisans' work alive. Visitors are invited to watch the craftspeople at work.

Open June through September, Monday through Friday 7 to 5, Saturday from 8, Sunday from noon; October through May, Monday through Friday 7 to 5. **Directions:** From the center of town, take the road to the right of the town hall. Rowantrees is next to Blue Hill Inn. (207) 374-5535.

The Young Fool Renaissance Fair, Rowantrees Pottery. 2-day juried crafts fair, sponsored by Maine State Council on Arts and Humanities and Rowantrees Pot-

Two-cup teapot on matching trivet, Rowantrees Pottery, Blue Hill

tery, and usually held during the first weekend of August; call to verify dates. Hours: 10 to 5. About 40 professional and amateur craftspeople exhibit pottery, stained glass, turned wood, and other crafts. Demonstrations of spinning, turned wood, and stained glass. Many exhibitors attend in Renaissance costumes. Food and entertainment available. 2,500 to 3,500 visitors annually. Admission charge. (207) 374-2782.

To get to Boothbay Harbor, take Route 1 east through Wiscasset, then turn south on Route 27. Continue on Route 27 about 12 miles to the center of town.

BOOTHBAY HARBOR

The Left Bank, Atlantic and Bay streets (Richard Macdonald, Lobster Cove), 04538. Macdonald sells his own contemporary stained glass, including lights, sconces, boxes, and larger works for walls and windows. He also carries the works of other craftspeople. Prices range from $10 to $500. "All pieces are exceptionally solid in construction. My long-term involvement in New England crafts has enabled me to get work from some people who do not widely wholesale."

Open May 15 to October 15, Monday through Saturday 10 to 5; except month of August, when shop is open daily 10 to 9. **Directions:** From the center of town, take Union Street to Atlantic Avenue, which goes to the left (east) side of the harbor. (207) 633-4815 (studio), or 633-5228 (shop).

Mung Bean, 55 Townsend Avenue, 04538. Professional and amateur. Offered are unique, functional porcelain and stoneware; sterling silver, gold, and brass jewelry; sweaters, socks, and hats of Maine wool; and silk-screened, pen-and-ink, and scratchboard notes. Prices range from 25¢ to $500. Crafts are exclusively Maine made, stressing high quality and creativity.

Open month of June, daily 9:30 to 5:30; July and August, daily 9 AM to 9:30 PM; September and October, daily 9:30 to 5. **Directions:** The shop is in the center of town. (207) 633-5512.

Two's Company, 45 Commercial Street (Box 500), 04538. Professional. Shop features Maine-made pot holders, quilts, Boothbay flea bags of canvas and quilted calico, and prints and paintings by Maine artists. Prices range from 95¢ to $400.

Open mid-May through June, daily 10 to 5; July and August, daily 9 AM to 10 PM; September through mid-October, daily 10 to 6; mid-October to Christmas, Thursday through Sunday tentatively 10 to 5. **Directions:** From Route 27, stay right on Oak Street, then proceed downhill to Commercial Street. (207) 633-4821.

To get to Bridgton, take Route 302 or 17 to the center of town.

BRIDGTON

The Cool Moose, 102 Main Street, 04009. Professional. Shop offers handmade leather goods and silk-screened

T-shirts. Leather belts are a specialty. Prices range from $5 to $25. "We are the oldest handmade-leather shop in the state."

Open June through Labor Day, Monday through Saturday 10 to 5. **Directions:** The shop is on Route 302. (207) 647-2446.

Craftworks, 53 Main Street, 04009. Professional. Shop features pottery, baskets, and jewelry. Prices range from $5 to $500. Craftworks is located in an historic old church.

Open June through September, daily 10 to 9. **Directions:** The shop is on Route 302, downtown. (207) 647-5436.

BROOKLIN

Brooklin Craft Cooperative, Route 175 (Box 11), 04616. Professional. The cooperative offers a large variety of wood-fired, salt-glazed stoneware, as well as traditionally glazed stoneware and porcelain. Also carries hand-woven rugs and coverlets, silk-screened cards and T-shirts, and batik and hand-woven clothing. Prices range from 50¢ to $500. All crafts sold are the work of co-op members, craftspeople of Hancock County. Much of their work is produced on the premises.

Open June through September, Tuesday through Saturday 10 to 5; October through December, Thursday through Saturday 10 to 5; January and February, by appointment; March through May, Thursday through Saturday 10 to 5. **Directions:** From Route 1 in Bucksport, follow Route 175 southeast to the center of Brooklin. (207) 359-2124.

CAMDEN

To get to Camden, take Route 1 or 90.

Annual Arts and Crafts Show, Bok Amphitheatre and Atlantic Avenue. 1-day juried crafts fair, sponsored by Rockport-Camden-Lincolnville Chamber of Commerce (Box 246, 04843) and held the third Sunday in July. Hours: 9 to 4. More than 80 professional craftspeople and artists exhibit many crafts in and around the amphitheater, in a natural setting overlooking the harbor. 5,000 visitors annually. Admission free. **Directions:** From Route 1 in town, turn onto Atlantic Avenue by the public library. The fair site is just past the main street. (207) 236-4404.

Gallery Shop of Camden, 82 Elm Street, 04843. Professional. Shop features metal sculpture by Peter Weil, stained glass by Richard Macdonald, porcelain by Dottie Palmer, and silk-screened scarves by Stell and Shevis. Prices range from $5 to $195. The Gallery Shop carries the works of Maine craftspeople. Many items are one of a kind.

Open March through January, Monday through

Laminated-wood lamp base by Dennis Berger, Perspectives, Camden

Saturday 10 to 5. **Directions:** The shop is on Route 1, about ¼ mile from downtown and the harbor. (207) 236-4290.

Laurie V. Adams, Porcelain and Stoneware Pottery, Upper Mountain Street, 04843. Professional. Adams specializes in functional stoneware and porcelain pieces such as walls, reliefs, and tiles. Prices range from $5 to $200. This small shop offers personalized service, and both limited-production and one-of-a-kind pottery.

Open all year, Monday through Friday by appointment. **Directions:** The shop is on Route 52, about 1½ miles north of the village. (207) 236-8457.

Perspectives, 4 Bay View Street, 04843. Professional. Selections include functional and sculptural pottery; brass and silver jewelry; fabric handbags, clothing, and sculpture; batik wall hangings, pillows, and bags; and metal tools, sconces, and candle holders. Prices range from $4 to $250. "We are a cooperative of local craftspeople. We tend the shop ourselves and are always available to answer questions about our work."

Open July and August, daily 9:30 to 5:30, except Friday open to 9; September through December, Monday through Saturday 9:30 to 5; January through June, Tuesday through Saturday 9:30 to 5. **Directions:** From Route 1 in the center of town, turn onto Bay View Street. Perspectives is the second store on the left. (207) 236-8470.

Unique 1, 2 Bay View Street (Box 744), 04843. Professional. Shop specializes in sweaters hand knitted from 100% natural Maine wool. Prices range from $5 to $85. All knits are designed and produced in town.

Open September through June, Monday through Saturday 9 to 5; July and August, daily 9 to 9. **Directions:** From Route 1 in the center of town, turn onto Bay View Street. The shop is the first building on the left. (207) 236-8717.

CAPE PORPOISE

Hedgerow Baskets Studio, Grace Amoroso, Ward Road Extension (RFD 2, Box 959, Kennebunkport, 04046). Professional. Amoroso specializes in hand-woven baskets of sea grass, native Maine vines, and reeds. Prices range from $1.50 to $50.

Open all year, by appointment only. (207) 967-3430.

CASTINE

Studio Pottery, Court Street (Box 401), 04421. Professional. Shop owner-potter Dennis Riley produces functional, decorated porcelain pottery on the premises. His line includes dinner sets and cooking ware with original designs. Prices range from $5 to $100.

Open all year, by appointment only. **Directions:** From Route 1 in Orland, follow Route 175 south to Route 166A. Then take Route 166A to Castine. (207) 326-4077.

CENTER LOVELL

Kezar Lake Handcrafters, Route 5, 04016. Professional and amateur. Selections include pillows in crewel, patchwork, and quilted designs; copper enameled dishes and jewelry; wooden ware; bird houses; macramé; scrimshaw; dolls; dried-flower arrangements; water colors; pottery; quilts; and hangings. Also Christmas ornaments, decorative slates, ski sweaters and hats, and weavings. Prices range from 50¢ to $195. "Our handcrafts are made by New England's finest artisans, and are of a variety not found in other shops."

Open May through October, Monday through Saturday 10 to 5; November and December, Thursday through Saturday 10 to 5. **Directions:** From the Maine Turnpike just north of Gray, follow Route 26 north to Norway, then Route 118 west to Lynchville. From Lynchville, head south on Route 5. (207) 925-1665.

CHERRYFIELD

Ricker Blacksmith Shop, Ridge Road (Box 50A), 04622. Professional. Shop owner George Brace creates and sells wrought-iron tables, spiral staircases, andirons, fireplace screens, and fireplace tools. Prices begin at $10. The shop is the "oldest continuously run family blacksmith shop in the Northeast."

Open all year, Monday through Friday 8 to 5, Saturday to noon. **Directions:** Follow Route 1 about 30 miles north of Ellsworth to Cherryfield; then take the first right after the bridge and go ½ mile to the shop, which is on the right. (207) 546-7954.

CORNISH

Pineledge Studio Shop, Durgintown Road, 04020. Professional. Shop features reverse glass painting for antique mirrors, clocks, and frames; hand-chased pewter and sterling silver bracelets, pendants, and earrings; and costumed apple-head and pomegranate dolls. Custom orders accepted for illuminated Old English initials and on New England fraktur including birth and marriage records, bookmarks, and illuminated calligraphy. Prices range from $3 to $400. All items in the shop are meticulously designed and created by Ralph

Oil lamp, Lovell Pewter, Damariscotta

To get to Damariscotta, take Route 1. Damariscotta is about 55 miles northeast of Portland.

and Mariette Berry.

Open by appointment or chance, but best to phone ahead. **Directions:** Take Maine Turnpike exit 8 to Portland, then Route 25 west about 30 miles to town. From Route 25, follow South Hiram Road one mile to Durgintown Road. Studio is 900 feet ahead. (207) 625-3324.

CUMBERLAND

United Maine Crafts Fair, Cumberland Fair Grounds, Blanchard Road. 3-day crafts fair, sponsored by United Maine Craftsmen (P.O. Box 861, Portland, 04104) and held during the second weekend of August. Hours: Friday and Saturday 10 to 8, Sunday 10 to 5. Over 230 professional and amateur craftspeople exhibit and demonstrate early American crafts such as candles, caning, ceramics, weaving, and woodworking. 10,000 visitors annually. Admission charge. **Directions:** Take Interstate 95 exit 10 onto routes 26 and 100. Then follow signs to the fairgrounds.

DAMARISCOTTA

Cove Lane Designs, Bristol Road (Box 336), 04543. Professional. Shop specializes in paintings done on old roofing slates and mounted on painted, antiqued pine board. Subjects are mostly marine scenes, seascapes, and New England bird life. Prices range from $10 to $45.

Open April through December, weekdays 10 to 4:30, sometimes weekends; during winter, by appointment. **Directions:** From Route 1, turn onto Bristol Road toward Bristol and Pemaquid. Turn right onto Cove Lane after the eighth building. The shop is on the corner of Cove Lane and Bristol Road. (207) 563-3873 after 5:30 PM.

Lovell Pewter, Schooner Wharf, 04543. Professional. Shop features pewter pieces such as hollowware, unusual trivets, butter molds, trays, oil lamps, cups, tankards, porringers, and Shaker bowls. Prices range from $6.50 to $450. All pewter is hand crafted in original designs.

Open all year, Monday through Saturday 9 to 5. **Directions:** Just off business Route 1 (Main Street) in town.

Thompsons Studio, Inc., Back Meadow Road, 04543. Professional. Tom Thompson specializes in gold jewelry, often incorporating gemstones into his pieces. Also carries tea services, candlesticks, porringers, and children's cups. Ernest Thompson Sr.'s etchings, oils, and water colors are also available. Prices range from $20 to $4,500. Tom Thompson's sensitivity to color, design, and texture in pewter results in "unique pieces made according to clients' needs and tastes." The studio is located in an old barn filled with tools of the trade, many of which are two hundred years old.

Open all year, Monday through Friday 10 to 5, Saturday to 3. **Directions:** Head north on Route 1 about 2 miles past town, and look for signs, which are posted about 1 mile past the Clarissa Illsley Tavern; then bear right. (207) 563-5280.

The Victorian Stable, Water Street, 04543. Professional and amateur. Selections include enamels, pewter, batik, carved birds, pottery, weavings, rugs, dolls, and jewelry. Prices range from $2 to $200. The work of over one hundred Maine craftspeople is featured here. Crafts are displayed in an attractive setting in an unusual and historic structure — a stable containing the original box stalls and tack room.

Open June through September, Monday through Saturday 10 to 5; other times, by appointment. **Directions:** From the Gulf station on Main Street in the center of town, turn right onto Water Street. (207) 563-3810, or 563-3880.

DEER ISLE

To get to Deer Isle, take Route 1 to Route 15, then take Route 15 south.

Hance Pottery/The Weave Shop, Route 15 (RFD 1, Box 91), 04627. Professional. Shop specializes in woven garments, accessories, and rugs. Also featured are flameware pottery (stovetop clay cookware), stoneware, and porcelain. Prices range from $5 to $500.

Open in two locations — Deer Isle village, November through mid-May, Monday through Friday 10 to 5; the Hance home, mid-May through October, daily 10 to 6. **Directions:** The shop is above Barter Hardware Store in the village, about 4 miles from Deer Isle Bridge. The Hance home is also located on Route 15, about 1 mile from the bridge. (207) 348-2883.

The Lawtons — Muriel and Don, 364 Reach Road, 04627. Professional. The Lawtons offer pottery, glass, lanterns, weaving, jewelry, and shell mobiles. All crafts are created by this husband-and-wife team. Prices range from $1 to $150. The Lawtons' specialty is the use of natural materials. The studio and gallery are located in two barns.

Open June through September, daily 10 to 5; October through May, by chance or appointment. **Directions:** From Route 15 in town, go over the bridge and causeway, then up the hill and around the curve (about ¼ mile). Reach Road is on the left; the studio and gallery are in the sixth house on the right. (207) 348-2244.

Once Upon an Island, Route 15 (50 Meadowbrook Road, Bangor, 04401). Selections include appliquéd clothing, quilts, and accessories. Also carries porcelain and other pottery, paintings, and jewelry. Prices range from $10 to $2,500. Once Upon an Island features variety, quality, and personalized articles.

47

Open May and June, weekends only; July and August, daily 10 to 6; September and October, weekends only. **Directions:** Heading south on Route 15, take the first left after the causeway. (207) 348-6057.

EAST BOOTHBAY

The Andersen Studio, Route 96 (Andersen Road), 04544. Professional. Brenda and Weston Andersen feature stoneware: sculptured birds and other animals, bowls, trays, platters, vases, and Chinese stone sculptures. Prices range from $2 to $200. The unique shapes offered are cast from original molds.

Open all year, daily 9 to 5. **Directions:** From Route 1 in Wiscasset, take Route 27 toward Boothbay Harbor. At the First National Bank, turn left onto Route 96 (Main Street), and continue about 2½ miles. The shop is on the left. (207) 633-4397.

ELLSWORTH

Strong Craft Gallery, Bar Harbor Road, 04605. Professional and amateur. Featured here is the work of over two hundred craftspeople. Pottery is a specialty, but glass, wood, metal, jewelry, etchings, and water colors are also sold. Prices range from $5 to $150.

Open September through May, Monday through Saturday 9 to 5; June through August, Monday through Friday 9 to 9, Saturday 9 to 6, Sunday 11 to 6. **Directions:** The shop is on Route 3, between the center of Ellsworth and Bar Harbor. (207) 667-2595.

FRANKLIN

Hog Bay Pottery/Susanne Grosjean, Weaving, Route 200, 04634. Professional. Shop features Charles Grosjean's place settings, kitchenware, and serving pieces in stoneware and porcelain; also Susanne Grosjean's hand-woven fabrics and hand-spun yarn for knitting and weaving. Prices range from $5 to $50 for pottery, and from $50 to $350 for woven goods.

Open June through September, Monday through Saturday 10 to 4; October through May, variable hours — please call ahead. **Directions:** From Route 1 near Sullivan harbor, turn onto Route 200, and go 4 miles toward Franklin. The shop is just beyond East Franklin, on the left. (207) 565-2282.

To get to Freeport, take Interstate 95 to the Freeport exit, then take Route 1 (which becomes Main Street) into town.

FREEPORT

Brown Goldsmiths, 1 Mechanic Street, 04032. Professional. Steve and Judy Brown, a husband-and-wife team, specialize in fine jewelry in various colors of the karat golds. Diamonds and colored gems are set in one-of-a-kind pieces. The work includes forged, fabricated, cast, and crocheted pieces. Prices begin at $25. Shop is located in the town's old Masonic Hall; the Browns work on the premises.

Open all year, Tuesday through Saturday 10 to 5. **Directions:** The shop is just off Main Street, 1 block from the L.L. Bean store. (207) 865-6263.

The Decoy Shop, 10 South Street (Box E), 04032. Professional. Shop specializes in hand-crafted decoys, both decorative and functional. Lamps and other home accessories are also sold. Prices range from $25 to $150.

Open all year, Monday through Friday 9 to 4. **Directions:** From Main Street in the center of town, turn onto Bow Street (across from L.L. Bean store). Cross the tracks and turn right onto South Street. The shop is approximately 100 yards ahead. (207) 865-6722.

Praxis Fine Crafts, 136 Main Street, 04032. Professional. Crafts cooperative sells stoneware, porcelain, and flameware pottery; stained glass; woodwork; hand-woven clothing and wall hangings; sterling silver, gold, and "married metal" jewelry; and leather goods. Other items for sale include hand-woven throw rugs, canvas bags, and luggage. Prices range from $5 to $1,000. The works of thirteen of "Maine's finest professional craftspeople" are displayed here, with the craftspeople themselves exhibiting their wares. The artisans are glad to explain how various items are made and should be cared for.

Open July through December, daily 10 to 6; January through June, Monday through Saturday 10 to 6. **Directions:** The shop is on Main Street, 3 blocks north of the L.L. Bean store. (207) 865-6201.

Dogwood pin in fourteen-karat gold by Steve and Judy Brown, Brown Goldsmiths, Freeport

GORHAM

Country Weave Shed, Dunlap Road (RFD 2), 04038. Professional. Mary and Ernest Wyman specialize in hand-woven goods such as rugs, stoles, baby blankets, and fabrics. Prices range from $1 to $75.

Open all year, "whenever we are home" — please phone ahead. (207) 892-4534.

GOULDSBORO

Maine Kiln Works, Highway 186 (Box 60), 04607. Professional. The Kiln Works specializes in stoneware pottery, including dinnerware sets, serving pieces, casseroles, mugs, wood-lid canisters, and jars. Also carries handmade quilts, wall hangings, lap quilts, and spreads. Some special orders accepted. Prices range from $2 to $200 for pottery, and from $100 to $400 for quilts. Owners Dan and Mary Lou Weaver produce all pottery and quilted work themselves.

Open all year, Monday through Saturday 9 to 5; except closed two weeks in the spring. **Directions:** Head north on Route 1 about 18 miles past Ellsworth, then turn right onto Highway 186 at the sign that reads "Schoodic Point section — Acadia National Park." Continue ½ mile to the shop. (207) 963-5819.

HALLOWELL

Earthly Delights, 81 Water Street, 04347. Professional and amateur. Shop carries hand-carved slate reliefs, hand-formed pottery figurines, leaded-glass windows, boxes, suncatchers, and lights. Also Maine-wool hats, scarves, vests, and mittens; marquetry; and hand-crafted silver jewelry. Items cost $10 to $65 and up. Earthly Delights carries the works of over two hundred Maine and other New England craftspeople.

Open February through December, Monday through Saturday 10 to 5. **Directions:** Take Interstate 95 north to exit 15 (Gardiner), then turn north onto Route 201. The shop is on Route 201. (207) 622-9801.

To get to Kennebunkport, take Route 1 north to Route 9, then take Route 9 east to Route 35. Take Route 35 into town.

KENNEBUNKPORT

Crafts on the Green, Ocean Avenue. 2-day juried crafts fair, sponsored by The School Around Us (04046) and held during the last weekend of July. Hours: 9:30 to 4. About 60 professional and amateur craftspeople and artists exhibit porcelain and other pottery, leaded stained glass windows and unusual room decorations, clay goods, ornaments, silk-screened totes and T-shirts, and shingled doll houses. Pottery is demonstrated. Admission free. **Directions:** Once in town, watch for colorful banners in Dock Square. (207) 646-7421.

Goose Rocks Pottery, Ocean Avenue (Goose Rocks Road), 04046. Professional. Owners Mary Lou Van Koehler and Bob Lipkin specialize in a wide range of functional handmade porcelain and stoneware pottery — oil lamps, planters, honey pots, vases, dinner plates with carved designs, and whimsical, brightly painted, carved boxes. Prices range from $3.50 to $150.

Open month of June, Friday through Monday 10 to 5; July and August, daily 10 to 5; month of September, Friday through Monday 10 to 5. **Directions:** The shop is located 1 mile down Ocean Avenue from Dock Square. (207) 967-2105.

The Pascos, Ocean Avenue (Box 427), 04046. Professional. Selections include silver jewelry, enameled copper sculptured birds, wrought-iron sculptures, rare hardwood plates, hand-turned trays, blown glass, stoneware, and porcelain. Also hand-woven neckties, blankets, scarves, skirt lengths, jacket lengths, stoles, throws, and car rugs. Prices range from $10 to $400.

Open May and June, Tuesday through Saturday 10 to 5; July and August, Monday through Saturday 9:30 to 5:30; month of September, Monday through Saturday 10 to 5; October through December, Tuesday through Saturday 10 to 5. **Directions:** In the center of town, turn onto Ocean Avenue. The shop is .2 mile ahead, on the right. (207) 967-4722.

The Wee Spinnaker, Ocean Avenue, 04046. Professional and amateur. Shop features crib toys, cradles, soft sculptures, pillows, Beatrix Potter lamps and mirrors, dolls and doll houses, stuffed animals, carved birds, paintings, ornaments, and herb wreaths. Prices range from $1 to $175. Over four hundred people from all over the country "make unusual items of very high quality" for The Wee Spinnaker.

Open mid-May through June, daily 10 to 5; July through Labor Day, daily 10 to 10; day after Labor Day through mid-October, daily 10 to 5. **Directions:** The shop is part of the Landing Hotel.

KINGFIELD

Once Upon an Island, Village West (50 Meadowbrook Road, Bangor, 04401). Professional and amateur. Selections include appliquéd clothing, quilts, and accessories. Also carries porcelain and other pottery, paintings, and jewelry. Prices range from $10 to $2,500. Once Upon an Island features variety, quality, and personalized articles.

Open November through April, daily 10 to 5. **Directions:** Take the Maine Turnpike exit onto Route 27, then follow Route 27 north to town and Sugarloaf Mountain. Village West is located on the mountain. (207) 237-2293.

LEWISTON

A.J. Flies, 53 Old Lisbon Road, 04240. Professional. Shop specializes in fishing flies, both single and assortments, and also carries feathered jewelry. Prices range from 70¢ to $13. The feathered jewelry is unique and conservative.

Open all year, weekdays 5 PM to 8 PM, some weekends. **Directions:** Take Interstate 95 exit 13, then go right to Reliable Oil Company. Turn left, then left again, and go ½ mile to the shop. (207) 782-5051 after 5 PM.

LINCOLNVILLE

Maine's Massachusetts House Shop and Gallery, Route 1, 04849. Professional. Selections include pottery, woodcarvings, silk-screened items, copper and steel weather vanes, gold and silver jewelry, and sculp-

Bas-relief carving of starboat, Maine's Massachusetts House Shop and Gallery, Lincolnville

tures. Prices range from $5 to $2,000.

Open all year, Monday through Saturday 9 to 5; Memorial Day to Columbus Day, also Sunday noon to 5. **Directions:** The shop is midway between Camden and Belfast. (207) 789-5705.

LOVELL

Arts and Artisans Fair, Route 5, the village. 1-day crafts fair, sponsored by the Charlotte Hobbs Library (04051) and held the third Saturday in August. Hours: 10 to 4. About 40 professional craftspeople and artists exhibit pottery, weaving, pewter, jewelry, spinning, quilting, blacksmithing, stained glass, miniature Shaker furniture, water colors, drawings, photography, appliqué, and hand knits. Spinning and basketry are demonstrated. The fair is held on the lawn of a school. Food booths. Admission free. **Directions:** From the Maine Turnpike in Westbrook, take Route 302 west to Fryeburg, then Route 5 north about 12 miles to Lovell. (207) 925-2946.

MACHIAS

Machias Arts and Craft Festival, Center Street. 1-day juried crafts festival, sponsored by Machias Arts and Craft Festival, Inc. (Box 50A, Ridge Road, Cherryfield, 04622) and held the third Saturday in August. Hours: 10 to 5. Approximately 75 professional and amateur craftspeople exhibit wood inlay work, blacksmithing, leather, pottery, jewelry, dolls, furniture, stained glass, and photography. Most crafts are demonstrated. The festival is held in conjunction with the annual Blueberry Festival. Food available. 10,000 visitors annually. Admission free. **Directions:** Take Route 1 about 200 miles north of Portland to Machias. Approaching the center of town, follow signs to the festival. (207) 546-7954.

MILBRIDGE

Eastern Maine Crafts Co-op, Route 1 (Box 30, Cherryfield, 04622). Professional. The works of a small group of professionals who own and operate the gallery and shop are available here. Items include stoneware pottery; rugs and woven apparel; cherry, walnut, and mahogany mirrors; metal sculpture; gold and silver jewelry with semiprecious stones; handmade quilts; blown glass; brass bells; and knitwear. Prices range from $5 to $500.

Open June through September, daily 10 to 5:30; mid-December to Christmas, daily 10 to 5:30. **Directions:** Follow Route 1 north about 30 miles beyond Ellsworth. The shop is on the western edge of

Milbridge; watch for a white frame house marked by a large black-and-yellow sign. (207) 546-2063, or 546-2269.

Porcelain bottle by Ken and Pax Vogt, The Clay Studio, Penobscot

NEWFIELD

Barnswallow Pottery, Main Street, 04056. Professional. Shop features high-fired, functional stoneware pottery, designed for use in the home and garden. Prices range from $2 to $20. All work is created in a century-old barn shop by owner Barbara Mostrom.

Usually open all year, daily 9 to 6; please call ahead. **Directions:** From Interstate 95 just north of Biddeford, take Route 5 west to Limerick. From Limerick, head south on Route 11. The shop is off Route 11, and is adjacent to the Willowbrook museum. (207) 793-8044.

NEW PORTLAND

Nowetah's American Indian Craft and Gift Shop, Route 27 (Box 14), 04954. Professional and amateur. Nowetah Timmerman offers handmade Indian items such as beadwork jewelry, rugs, mats, saddle blankets, leatherwork, and hand-embroidered Indian dresses. Items cost $1 to $40 and more, with most under $10. Only genuine pieces crafted by other Indians in the United States and Canada are featured, in addition to those made by Timmerman, a Cherokee-Susquehanna Indian.

Open all year, Monday through Saturday 10 to 5, Sunday from 1; in summer, sometimes evenings. **Directions:** From Interstate 95 in Augusta, head north on Route 27 about 55 miles. The shop is off Route 27, on an 800-foot-long scenic drive with a large parking turn-around. Watch for large dark-brown-and-yellow signs. (207) 628-4981.

OAKLAND

Meader Stoneware, Fairfield Street (Route 2, Box 280), 04963. Professional. Shop specializes in handmade stoneware, both functional and decorative. Popular items are unique stoneware masks, face mugs, and leg planters. Most pieces are made on the premises. Hand-woven goods are also offered. Prices range from $2 to $60.

Open July, August, and December, daily 9 to 6; May, June, and September through November, usually same hours, but please call. **Directions:** Take Interstate 95 Waterville/Oakland exit, then head west 3 miles to town and Route 23. The shop is on Route 23, about 1¼ miles north of town. (207) 465-7790.

To get to Ogunquit, take Interstate 95 exit 1 (York/Ogunquit), then turn left onto Route 1. Or, take Interstate 95 exit 2 and turn right onto Route 1. To reach Perkins Cove, turn onto Shore Road from Route 1 (Main Street) in town, and follow signs.

OGUNQUIT

Maple Hill Pottery Craft Gallery, Perkins Cove, 03907. Professional. Offered here is a variety of crafts from 14-karat gold and sterling silver jewelry to hand-woven rugs, clothing, and baskets. Also sold is pottery made by the shop owner. Prices begin at $5. The crafts are one-of-a-kind products. Craftspeople from all over the United States are represented.

Open Memorial Day weekend to Labor Day weekend, daily 10 to 10. (207) 646-2134.

The Strawberry Bazaar, Perkins Cove, 03907. Professional and amateur. Shop features hand-thrown pottery, vases, planters, and oil lamps, and hand-formed figurines. Also carries metal wall sculptures, silk-screened wall prints, and jewelry in gold, silver, and bronze. Prices range from $2 to $200.

Open Memorial Day through Columbus Day: spring and fall, daily 10 to 5; summer, daily 10 to 10. **Directions:** The shop is opposite the footbridge in Perkins Cove. (207) 646-5205.

The Unicorn Handcraft Shop, Cliff House Motel grounds, Shore Road (Box 1266), 03907. Professional and amateur. Selections include blown glass, puppets, glass etchings, primitives, photography, unicorns, handbags, quilts, scarves, and bells. Prices range from $2.50 to $250. Featured are American crafts only.

Open mid-May through mid-October, daily 9 to 6. **Directions:** From Main Street, follow Shore Road 3 miles to the Cliff House Motel. (207) 646-5786.

ORLAND

H.O.M.E., Inc., Route 1 (Box 408), 04472. Professional and amateur. Shop features quilts, dolls, pottery, hand-woven materials, wooden ware, pot holders, toys, and jewelry. Prices range from 50¢ to $175. The shop stocks Maine handcrafts only, with a choice of over two hundred items. H.O.M.E. is a non-profit organization "designed to bring additional income to Maine's rural, elderly, and low-income people."

Open January through April, Monday through Friday 9 to 5, May through December daily 9 to 5. **Directions:** The shop is about 125 miles north of Portland, 4 miles east of Bucksport, and about 17 miles west of Ellsworth. (207) 469-7961.

PENOBSCOT

The Clay Studio (Star Route, Box 20), 04476. Professional. Ken and Pax Vogt specialize in wheel-thrown porcelain and stoneware pottery, including their complete line of oven-proof dinnerware. Prices range from $5 to $200. All work is done on the premises. The Vogts pay careful attention to the details of each finished product, and most pieces are one of a kind.

Open all year, Monday through Saturday 9:30 to 4:30. **Directions:** Take Route 1 east for 5 miles beyond Bucksport to Route 15, then head southeast on Route 15 for 3½ miles to Route 199. Turn right onto Route 199 and go 3½ miles to the studio. (207) 326-8273.

Patchwork and appliqué doll by Nancy Abbott, The Marketplace, Portland

PHILLIPS

The Natural Choice, Route 4 (Box 212), 04966. Professional and amateur. Selections include all-wool hand-braided rugs and hand-woven goods such as shawls, scarves, and place mats. Also offers dried-flower arrangements, straw wreaths with dried flowers, hand-thrown pottery, leather goods, potpourri, baskets, canvas bags, and pillows. Prices range from 65¢ to $130. All crafts are the work of local craftspeople.

Open mid-May through December, Monday through Saturday 9 to noon and 12:30 to 5. **Directions:** Take the Maine Turnpike exit 12 in Augusta, to Route 4. Then head north on Route 4 about 65 miles to Phillips. The shop is 500 feet beyond the Texaco station. (207) 639-2994.

PORTLAND

Maine Potters Market, 9 Moulton Street, 04111. Professional. Shop/gallery is operated on a cooperative basis and features the works of seventeen Maine potters who live and work in various parts of the state from the Allagash to the outer islands. Prices range from $3 to $100.

Open all year (except usually closed February), Monday through Saturday 10 to 5, plus some evenings in summer. **Directions:** The shop/gallery is in the Old Port Exchange, at the bottom of Exchange Street, between Fore and Commercial streets. (207) 744-1633.

The Marketplace, Inc., 101 Exchange Street, 04101. Professional and amateur. Shop specializes in Maine crafts such as Indian baskets, quilts, wooden folk toys, pottery using native clay and glazes, Shaker herbs, potpourri, and Maine yarns. Prices range from $1 to $500. "We emphasize service and special orders, which often means considerable research."

Open January through April, Monday through Saturday 9:30 to 5:30, except Thursday open to 8; May through December, Monday through Saturday 9 to 6, plus Thursday to 8. **Directions:** The Marketplace is 1 block down Exchange Street from Congress Street. (207) 774-1376.

To get to Portland and the Old Port Exchange, take the Maine Turnpike to Interstate 295. Take Interstate 295 exit 7 onto Route 1A. At the fourth traffic light, turn right onto Congress Street and go 3 blocks, then turn left onto Exchange Street.

Stoneware chime clock with quartz movement, Ron Burke, Shapleigh

SEARSPORT

Knyvetta Gallery of Fine Arts and Crafts, Route 1, 04974. Professional and amateur. Selections include paintings, marquetry, woodwork, quilts, photography, knitted goods, and toys. Other featured items include crocheted goods, macramé, ceramics, graphics, and handmade clothing. Prices range from $2 to $200. Knyvetta is an old country schoolhouse; the shop is on the first floor, the gallery on the second.

Open June 15 through October 15 (or through fall foliage season), Thursday through Tuesday 9:30 to 4:30. (Days open are subject to change.) **Directions:** The gallery is 2 miles north of Searsport, which is about 110 miles north of Portland. (207) 548-2291.

SHAPLEIGH

Ron Burke, Butler's Corner Road (RR 1, Box 325, Springvale, 04083). Professional. Studio specializes in abstract landscape and seascape clocks, and stoneware wall clocks. Prices range from $20 to $75.

Open all year, by appointment only. **Directions:** Take Route 109 five miles north of Sanford, then turn right onto Butler Corner Road; the shop is 1½ miles down. Shapleigh is approximately 40 miles from both Portland and Portsmouth, New Hampshire. (207) 324-9540.

SOUTH PENOBSCOT

North Country Textiles, Route 175 (Box 176), 04476. Professional. Shop specializes in hand-woven clothing, accessories, place mats, and pillows, all made of natural fibers. Prices range from $3.50 to $250.

Open mid-June through mid-September, Tuesday through Saturday 10 to 5; rest of year, by appointment. **Directions:** Take Route 1 to Bucksport, then head south on Route 175. The shop is at the junction of routes 175 and 177. (207) 326-8222.

To get to South Thomaston, take Route 1 east through Thomaston, then turn south on Route 131. Or, from Rockland, take Route 73 south.

SOUTH THOMASTON

'Keag Pottery, Westbrook Street, 04858. Professional. Studio/showroom specializes in owner Anthony Oliveri's functional stoneware and porcelain, from salt and pepper shakers to entire place settings. Prices range from $3 to $50. Oliveri stresses simplicity of design, especially in his bold patterns of deep blue and dark brown on white.

Open June to Labor Day, Tuesday through Saturday 9 to 6, Sunday from noon, Monday by appointment; Labor Day through May, by chance or appointment. **Directions:** Heading south on Route 131, turn left onto Westbrook Street. (207) 594-7915.

The Old Spalding House, Route 73 (Box 126), 04858. Professional. Shop features crafts from Maine only, "collected from the best Maine craftspeople." Pieces include pottery, prints, silk-screened goods, weaving, and batik. The shop is located in a carriage house attached to a Maine Gothic house built in 1845.

Open May through October, "with hours to accommodate the traveling public" — please call ahead; during winter, by appointment only. **Directions:** From Route 1 in Rockland, head south on Route 73 for 4 miles toward Spruce Head. The shop is on the right, in a gray house marked by a large white sign. (207) 594-7436.

SOUTH WINDHAM

Heritage Metalcraft, Route 202, 04082. Professional. Shop specializes in decorative metal products cast, forged, or hammered at the foundry and displayed in the shop. Offered are weather vanes, wall plaques, toys, utensils, furniture, and candlesticks. Prices range from $2.80 to $890. Emphasizes quality metal crafts, mostly in colonial and other early American motifs. Visitors are welcome to watch items being made.

Open all year, Monday through Saturday 9 to 5, Sunday from noon; except closed Christmas and Thanksgiving. **Directions:** Heading north on the Maine Turnpike, take exit 8 at Westbrook, then follow Route 302 to the rotary. From the rotary, take Route 202 south about 2 miles to the shop. (207) 892-6739.

STEUBEN

Peter Weil, Sculpture Studio, town green, 04680. Professional. Weil specializes in welded-steel and metal-sculpture figures. Also carries weather vanes, chandeliers, candle stands, and fireplace tools. Prices range from $10 to $300. All work is high quality, and features Weil's unique designs — "each piece is carefully finished and is a sculpture in its own right."

Open all year, Monday through Saturday, various hours — please phone ahead. **Directions:** Take Route 1 about 25 miles north of Ellsworth to Steuben. The house/studio is on old Route 1, opposite the post office and the church. (207) 546-2269.

STONINGTON

Green Head Forge, Old Quarry Road, 04681. Professional. Forge specializes in wrought-metal products — chandeliers, tables, fireplace sets, andirons, fire grates, signs, and brackets. Prices range from $10 to $15,000. Designs of all items are original.

To get to Stonington, take routes 1 and 3 to Route 15, then take Route 15 south. Route 15 becomes Main Street in Stonington.

Open April through December, Tuesday through Saturday 8 to 4; January through March, by appointment — phone at noon or write. **Directions:** Old Quarry Road is off West Main Street. (207) 367-2632.

The Purring Owl at Green Head Forge, Old Quarry Road, 04681. Shop features sterling silver jewelry, "featherweight" wrought-iron jewelry, "married metals" fabricated and forged in original designs, fanciful brass creatures, and small brass sculptures and hollow forms. Prices range from $10 to $200.

Open April through December, Tuesday through Saturday 8 to 4; January through March, by appointment — call before 8 AM or at noon, or write. (207) 367-2632.

Some Stuff (Co-op Gallery), 04681. Professional. Selections include pottery, metal, fiber, wood, glass, graphics, photography, paintings, and sculptures. Prices range from $1 to $1,000.

Open late May through Columbus Day, daily 9:30 to 5:30. **Directions:** The gallery is on Main Street. (207) 367-5006.

Wooden pencil cup, Harpswell House Gallery, Topsham

TOPSHAM

Harpswell House Gallery, 49 Winter Street, 04086. Professional. Gallery specializes in slate and wood office accessories. Other offerings include trivets, candle sconces, hanging planters, ice buckets, tiles, wine racks, and lazy Susans. Products featuring unique combinations of slate and wood are crafted on the premises.

Open all year, Monday through Saturday 10 to 5. **Directions:** From Interstate 95, exit onto Route 196. Follow Route 196 into town, then, at the second traffic light, turn right onto Winter Street. The gallery is about ½ mile ahead, on the right. (207) 725-7694.

UNION

Abbott-Wheat Country Studio (RFD 2), 04862. Professional. Studio features batik paintings, one-of-a-kind character dolls, designer clothing, wall hangings and banners, and soft sculptures. Commission work accepted from both individuals and corporations. Prices range from $15 to $3,000. Studio/gallery is located in a turn-of-the-century general country store.

Open all year, by appointment only. (207) 785-4656.

WALDOBORO

VanDerwerker Pottery, Friendship Road (RFD 3), 04572. Professional. Gerrit K. VanDerwerker specializes in stoneware and porcelain ovenware, bread and serving bowls, five-piece dinnerware sets, teapots, pitchers, and lidded storage bowls. Prices range from $5 to $50. Incorporated into VanDerwerker's pottery is "a sense of classical contemporary design, with the use of wood-ash and slip glazes."

Open all year, Monday through Saturday 9:30 to 5:30. **Directions:** Follow Route 1 north about 10 miles beyond Damariscotta, then turn south onto Route 220. The shop is on Friendship Road (Route 220), about 6 miles south of the village of Waldoboro. (207) 832-7061.

WATERVILLE

Silver Street Gallery, 18½ Silver Street, 04901. Professional. Selections include earrings, necklaces, and rings in silver, brass, and gold. Also carries functional and decorative pottery, stained-glass mirrors and windows, paintings, leather work, and wooden toys. Custom orders accepted for jewelry and stained glass. Prices range from $15 to $100. All crafts are made by Maine craftspeople living and working in the Waterville area.

Open all year, Monday through Saturday 11 to 5:30, except Friday open to 9; December 10 to Christmas, 10 to 9. **Directions:** Take Interstate 95 to Waterville exit. The gallery is 1 block off Main Street in the center of town, overlooking the shopping concourse. (207) 872-7581.

WEST BALDWIN

Mary's Applehead Characters, 57 Douglas Hill Road, 04091. Professional. Mary Blake creates 9-inch-tall, free-standing applehead dolls, fully dressed in colorful fabrics. Each of her dolls is one of a kind. Prices range from $18 to $25. Blake is devoted to "the rare traditional craft of applehead dolls, whose heritage can be traced back through colonial times to the American Indians."

Open all year, daily 9 to 5. **Directions:** Take Interstate 95 exit 8 at Westbrook, and follow Route 25 west to Route 113. Then head north on Route 113 toward West Baldwin. Douglas Hill Road is just off Route 113; a sign with directions is located 1½ miles up Douglas Hill Road. (207) 625-3529.

WISCASSET

The Friend, Main Street (Box 421), 04578. Professional and amateur. Shop features Hazel Hayden's quilts and calicos, as well as Jack Hayden's tinware — sconces, chandeliers, patterns, and plaques. Prices range from $1 to $400. Only the "best quality quilted items" are featured, "and our tinware is now sold as far away as Germany and Alaska."

Open all year, Monday through Saturday 9 to 5;

July and August, daily 9 to 5. **Directions:** The shop is in the center of Wiscasset, which is about 45 miles north of Portland. (207) 882-7806.

To get to Yarmouth, take the Interstate 95 Yarmouth exit, then follow Route 1 to Route 115, which is Main Street in Yarmouth. Or, take Route 88 along Casco Bay to town.

YARMOUTH

Martha Hall/Looms and Yarn, 46 Main Street, 04096. Professional. Shop specializes in Maine-wool sweaters, hats and mittens, hand-woven shawls, and alpaca scarves. Custom orders accepted. Prices begin at $12.50. The shop is housed in an old sea-captain's home, a National Historic Landmark.

Open all year, Monday through Saturday 10 to 5. **Directions:** The shop is on Main Street, across from a large stone church. (207) 846-9334.

The Pottery Shop, 7 Smith Street, 04096. Professional. Shop features hand-built and wheel-thrown stoneware and porcelain, with both functional and decorative pieces. Prices range from $5 to $100. All pottery in the shop is produced by husband-and-wife team Dick and Peg Miller in a barn studio on the premises.

Open all year, Monday through Saturday 9 to 5, Sunday by appointment. **Directions:** Follow Route 88 north along Casco Bay to town, then, after passing Westcustago Inn, take the first left (onto Smith Street). The studio is in the barn attached to the second house on the left. (207) 846-4981.

The Sign of the Owl, 198 Main Street, 04096. Professional and amateur. Shop features whimsical porcelain boxes by Nance Mooney, brass wind bells by Richard Fisher, tiny boxes with bronze decoys from Baekgaard, and three-dimensional scene boxes silk screened by R. Hasenfus. Prices average $10 to $15.

Open all year, Monday through Saturday 9:30 to 5; except August and December to 5:30; some Sundays in Christmas season. **Directions:** Take Interstate 95 Yarmouth exit, then follow signs to the shop, which is located in the Old Mill (next to the bridge) at the corner of Route 88 and Main Street (Route 115). (207) 846-4682.

YORK HARBOR

Annual Seacoast Crafts Fair, Route 1A (Box 25), 03909. A 3-day juried crafts fair held the last Thursday through Saturday of August. Hours: Thursday through Friday 10 to 8; Saturday 10 to 4. About 60 professionals and amateurs exhibit and demonstrate crafts selected for excellence of design and craftsmanship. This is an indoor fair in an air-conditioned building. Food available. 2,500 visitors annually. Admission charge. **Directions:** From Route 1, turn east onto Route 1A. The fair is held in Saint Christopher's auditorium, between York village and York Harbor. (207) 363-2397.

A *YANKEE* GUIDEBOOK

HANDCRAFT CENTERS

·OF NEW ENGLAND·

III.
Massachusetts

We found more crafts shops and events in Massachusetts than in any other state in New England. That's not unexpected; there are more *people* in Massachusetts. But if someone had taken a handful of confetti and sprinkled it on a map of the Bay State, he could hardly have distributed the area's craftspeople more evenly; from the North Shore to the tip of Cape Cod, from Boston to the Berkshires, there are clusters of crafts shops in virtually every section of the state — and that means if you live in or near Massachusetts, there are bound to be at least a few near you.

Candle castle by Gail Turner, Mill Stone Pottery, East Dennis (see page 78)

ACTON

Ann Thornton Pottery, 6 Kelley Road, 01720. Professional. Studio features a complete line of hand-thrown and hand-built, high-fired stoneware pottery. Prices range from $5 to $80. All work is done in the studio, and demonstrations are given. Custom orders accepted.

Open all year, Thursday through Saturday noon to 5, and by appointment. **Directions:** Heading east on Route 111, turn right onto Route 27 at the traffic light. Then take the second left, onto Kelley Road; the studio is in the second house on the left. (617) 263-0774.

Handworks, Inc., 452 Route 2A, 01720. Professional and amateur. Shop features hand-hewn glass, jewelry, ceramics, clothing, prints, furniture, and toys. Over 200 artisans from all over the United States are represented. Prices range from $5 to $1,500. A husband-and-wife team owns and operates the shop. "Great care and thought have been given to selecting merchandise to please many tastes."

Open all year, Monday through Saturday 10 to 5:30, Thursday to 9. **Directions:** Take Route 2 or Route 111 to Route 2A. (617) 263-1707.

"Motifs" of Family Works, 14 Newtown Road, 01720. Professional. Studio specializes in Carol Emerson's ceramic and porcelain items created from original molds, and in custom tiles. Prices range from $2 to $5.

"Open all the time." **Directions:** Newtown Road is off Route 27 in Acton center, near a large monument and the town hall. (617) 263-7238.

To get to Acton, take Route 495 exit 28 toward Boxborough, and go east on Route 111 to Route 27 or Route 2A. Or, from Route 128 go west on Route 2 to Route 2A or Route 27.

AMHERST

River Valley Crafts, 236 North Pleasant Street, 01002. Professional. Shop features ceramics in porcelain and stoneware; gold, silver, and fiber jewelry; blown glass; wood; and stained glass. Prices range from $5 to $500. One-of-a-kind pieces are made by craftspeople whose work is also displayed in the Metropolitan Museum, the Smithsonian, and the Chrysler Museum of Glass. More than one hundred craftspeople are represented.

Open all year, Monday through Saturday 10 to 5:30. **Directions:** From the Amherst common, take a left onto Route 116 north, which is North Pleasant Street. (413) 253-7919.

Silverscape Designs, 264 North Pleasant Street, 01002. Professional. Shop specializes in handmade jewelry using gems of every description, from amethysts to fire emeralds to certificate diamonds; also carries art glass from studios throughout the country, lamps, roll-top jewelry boxes, and handmade drums. Full repair service and restoration of antique jewelry

To get to Amherst, take Interstate 91 exit 19 and head east on Route 9 about seven miles to the Amherst common.

available. Prices range from $5 to $500, with most under $100. "The resident goldsmith is the owner and is generally in the store."

Open January through November, Monday through Saturday 10 to 6, except open Friday to 9; month of December, Monday through Saturday 10 to 9, Sunday noon to 5. **Directions:** From the Amherst common, turn onto Route 116 north, which is North Pleasant Street. Silverscape is 3½ blocks ahead, on the left. (413) 253-3324.

BARNSTABLE

Artisans Fall Festival, Barnstable Unitarian Church grounds, Route 6A and Hyannis Road, 02630. A 1-day juried crafts fair, sponsored by the church and held the first Saturday after Labor Day. Hours: 10 to 5. About 30 professional artists and craftspeople exhibit pottery, chair caning, water-color and oil painting, soft sculpture, stained and leaded glass, lapidary work and other jewelry, leather craft, and weaving. Some crafts are demonstrated. 600 to 700 visitors annually. Admission free. **Directions:** The church is at the junction of Route 6A and Hyannis Road (location of the only traffic light in the village). (617) 394-9845.

BELMONT

Donna Marie's Pots, 16 Coolidge Road, 02178. Professional. Donna Marie Arganbright specializes in white and brown functional stoneware pottery. Most pieces are wheel thrown, some hand built. Her selection includes casseroles, mugs, pitchers, sugar-and-cream sets, bowls, vases, and hurricane lamps. Prices range from $5 to $50. Features "a distinctive style, and a fresh, very functional folklore look. Some pieces are quite decorative, some handsomely simple."

Open all year; please call ahead. **Directions:** From Route 128, take exit 46A onto Route 2 east. Then take exit 2 to Route 60 in Belmont center. Turn right onto Route 60, and then left at the first traffic light (Pleasant Street). After the next traffic light, turn right onto Coolidge Road. (617) 489-2658.

"Rain Lady," soft sculpture, River Valley Crafts, Amherst

BILLERICA

Hymenoptera Potter/Jean Card, 43 Pond Street (47 Pond Street), 01821. Professional. Shop features wheel-thrown and press-molded, hand-built stoneware — decorative clocks, wall pockets, lamps, and mirrors. Also carries garden sculpture, including bird feeders and bird baths. Prices range from $5 to $200.

Open all year, various hours — please call for an appointment. **Directions:** From Interstate 495, take

Route 3 south then Route 129 to Pond Street south. The shop is at the corner of Pond Street and Pondover Road. Or, from Route 128, take exit 43 to Route 3 north to Billerica center; then follow Andover Road to Pond Street north. (617) 663-3079.

BOSTON

A.B.L.E.'s Handcrafts of New England, 152 State Street, 02109. Professional and amateur. Shop features afghans, nautical lamps, crocheted toys, dolls, pottery, jewelry, sweaters, hats, mittens, and wood inlays. Prices range from 65¢ to $200. A.B.L.E. is a VISTA non-profit store selling the work of low-income New England crafters. It is the only such program in the country that deals with a multi-state region.

Open all year, Monday through Saturday 10 to 9, Sunday noon to 6. **Directions:** The shop is across from the Custom House tower, in the Faneuil Hall Marketplace area. (617) 523-9096.

Alianza, 140 Newbury Street, 02108. Professional. Selections include innovative, contemporary American handcrafts — scenic quilts, stained-glass mirrors and boxes, blown-glass stemware and paperweights, functional ceramics, hand-wrought jewelry, and whimsical wall decorations. Prices range from $5 to $500.

Open all year, Monday through Saturday 10 to 6, except open Wednesday to 8. **Directions:** The shop is located between the Public Garden and Dartmouth Street. (617) 262-2385.

Annual 3D/Fine Arts Crafts Sale, Massachusetts College of Art, 364 Brookline Avenue, 02215. A 5-day juried crafts fair, sponsored by the 3D/Fine Arts Department of the college and held the week before Christmas. Hours: 9 to 5. About 100 student and professional faculty craftspeople exhibit and demonstrate ceramics, fibers, metalwork, and glass. "Objects range from the trivial to the exotic. The show/sale has become a tradition of pride for all parties entering it." Thousands of visitors annually. Admission free. **Directions:** Take Route 9 (Huntington Avenue) to Longwood Avenue, then turn west onto Longwood Avenue. The college is located on the corner of Brookline and Longwood avenues. (617) 731-2340.

Artisans Cooperative, 175 K. South Market, Faneuil Hall Marketplace (Box 216, Chadds Ford, PA 19317). Professional. Selections include traditional handmade quilts, stained glass, metalwork, wood, and baskets. Prices range from $2 to $700. Emphasizes the presentation and quality of crafts, the range of inventory, and artisan participation in the marketplace. Artisans Cooperative is a non-profit organization providing work and experience for rural craftspeople through the

To get to Boston, take Interstate 93 (Southeast Expressway) or Interstate 90 (Massachusetts Turnpike). To get to Newbury Street, take the Prudential/Copley Square exit from Interstate 90, turn left onto Dartmouth Street, and go past Boylston Street 1 block to Newbury Street; or, take the subway green line to Copley station. To get to Faneuil Hall Marketplace/waterfront area, take Interstate 93 south to the Haymarket exit or Interstate 93 north to the State Street exit; or, take the subway blue or green line to Government Center station.

production of hand-crafted items.

Open all year, Monday through Saturday 10 to 9, Sunday noon to 6. **Directions:** The shop is in the heart of Boston's restored marketplace. (617) 742-0938.

Ben Kupferman, Goldsmith/Designer/Sculptor, 115 Atlantic Avenue, 02110. Professional. Shop specializes in original, one-of-a-kind contemporary gold jewelry. Many pieces are on display. Kupferman also accepts custom work. Prices range from $200 to $5,000. The designer stresses the originality and quality of all items. He works "in full view of people wishing to see a piece of fine jewelry created before their eyes. The scope and content of my work set my shop apart from all others."

Open all year, Tuesday through Saturday 9:30 to 4. **Directions:** The shop is located in the Mercantile Building in the waterfront area, 5 minutes from the New England Aquarium. (617) 742-1982.

Boston Christmas Crafts Expo, Commonwealth Pier Exhibition Hall, Northern Avenue. 3-day juried crafts fair, sponsored by American Crafts Expositions, Inc. (Box 368, Canton, CT 06019) and held the weekend after Thanksgiving. Hours: Friday noon to 9, Saturday 10 to 9, Sunday 10 to 8. About 250 professional craftspeople exhibit and demonstrate a wide variety of crafts in many media. 25,000 visitors annually. Admission charge. **Directions:** Take the North Atlantic Avenue exit off the Southeast Expressway (Interstate 93); this becomes Northern Avenue. Go about 4 blocks to Commonwealth Pier. (203) 693-6311.

Rocking chair by Kingsley Brooks, Society of Arts and Crafts, Boston

Clay Critters Studio, 643 West Roxbury Parkway, 02132. Professional. Studio features hand-built clay animals, individually made without molds or throwing. Prices range from $35 to $150. Artisan Doris M. Duncan emphasizes the uniqueness, individuality, and character of each piece.

Open all year, Saturday and Sunday 10 to 6; weekdays by appointment. **Directions:** From Route 128, take Route 1 north 4 miles to Washington Street; go about 5½ miles, then turn left onto West Roxbury Parkway. After 1 mile, turn left onto Pelton Street, and then take a right back onto West Roxbury Parkway. (617) 325-5647.

John Lewis, Inc., 97 Newbury Street, 02116. Professional. Shop specializes in original designs in gold and silver jewelry. Prices range from $10 to $3,000.

Open all year, Tuesday through Saturday 10 to 5, plus open Wednesday to 7. **Directions:** The shop is located between the Public Garden and Dartmouth Street. (617) 266-6665.

Skylight Jewelers, 30 Bromfield Street, 02108. Professional. Shop specializes in gold and silver jewelry, designed and executed using fine and unusual gems. Prices range from $20 to $2,000. Skylight emphasizes a variety of styles in fine jewelry, "from art to classic."

Open all year, Monday through Friday 10 to 6, Saturday from noon. **Directions:** The shop is downtown, near the Park Street subway station, Filene's Department Store, and the Parker House restaurant. (617) 426-0521.

Society of Arts and Crafts, 175 Newbury Street, 02116. Professional. The Society features both a retail shop and an exhibition center, with tables and stands by Richard Tanner, wall clocks in wood cases by Ernest White, three-dimensional stained-glass constructions by Joseph Ferguson, both functional and decorative ceramics by Gerry Williams and Daisy Brand, three-dimensional fiber wall hangings by Lialand Teger, and brass kitchen implements by Jennifer Sayre. All items "are of quality suitable for gifts or prized personal possessions." Prices range from $10 to $4,000. The upstairs gallery is Boston's first exhibition center exclusively for the crafts.

Open all year, Tuesday through Friday 11 to 6, Saturday 10 to 5. (617) 266-1810.

Women's Educational and Industrial Union, 356 Boylston Street, 02116. Professional. Selections include a variety of hand-painted articles and decoupage; also dolls, children's quilts, and children's knitwear. Custom needlework done. Prices range from $5 to $100. "The Women's Educational and Industrial Union is a social-service organization that operates five shops for the benefit of its social-service programs."

Open September through June, Monday through Friday 9 to 5, Saturday from 10. **Directions:** Take Prudential/Copley Square exit from Interstate 90, and turn left onto Dartmouth Street, then right onto Boylston Street. The shop is on the right, across from the Public Garden. (617) 536-5651.

BOXBOROUGH

Craft Fair, Sheraton Inn and Conference Center, 01719. A 2-day juried crafts fair, sponsored by William Clark and held the Saturday and Sunday after Thanksgiving. Hours: 11 to 6. About 150 professional craftspeople exhibit jewelry, fiber, glass, leather, wood, and pottery. Demonstrations usually of blown glass, weaving, and painting (vary each year). 5,000 to 7,000 visitors annually. Admission charge. **Directions:** Take Interstate 495 to Route 111 east. A sign marking the Sheraton is a short distance ahead on the right. (617) 263-7243.

BREWSTER

A Thousand Patches Studio, 134 Thousand Oaks Drive, 02631. Professional. Studio specializes in twin-,

To get to Brewster, take Route 6 east to exit 9, 10, or 11.

standard-, and queen-sized quilts hand tufted in traditional designs such as log cabin, Dresden plate, and monkey wrench. Also carries patchwork quilts, and others in original designs. Prices range from $100 to $350. "Only the finest quality fabrics and batting are used."

Open April through December, by appointment only. (617) 896-7171.

Brewster Pottery, 437 Harwich Road (Box 888), 02631. Professional. Shop features hand-crafted stoneware and porcelain pottery, including wind chimes, planters, mugs, bowls, teapots, and bird feeders. Prices range from $5 to $100. Visitors may see pottery being made on the premises.

Open June through September, Monday through Saturday 9:30 to 6, Sunday from 1; off season, weekends by appointment. **Directions:** From Route 6 exit 10, turn left onto Route 124. Go 3¼ miles to the junction with Tubman Road. The shop is on the corner. (617) 896-3587.

Brooks Cards, 3732 Main Street, 02631. Professional. Shop specializes in personally designed and silk-screened Christmas cards and Cape Cod notes, the work of owner Gordon Brooks. Each card and note is imprinted to match the style of the message inside, and all messages are hand lettered. Cards are 20¢ apiece. All creative design and production are done by one person, and the cards are sold nowhere but in this shop.

Open July to Christmas, daily 10 to 5:30. **Directions:** The shop is on Route 6A, about 1 mile west of the Brewster/Orleans town line, and ½ mile east of the entrance to Nickerson State Park. (617) 255-1063.

The Lemon Tree Pottery, 1069 Route 6A, 02631. Professional. Shop features wheel-thrown and hand-built pottery; also carries scrimshaw, jewelry, stained glass, and whimsical stuffed dolls and animals. Prices range from $3.50 to $450. The "friendly atmosphere, good location, choice and quality of the work displayed, and our open courtyard" add to the ambiance of the shop.

Open April through December, Monday through Saturday 10 to 6, Sunday 1 to 5; January through March, Friday and Saturday 10 to 5, Sunday from 1. **Directions:** Take Route 6 exit 9, 10, or 11 to Route 6A, which parallels Route 6. (617) 896-3065.

Linda's Originals, 585 Slough Road, 02631. Professional. Linda Rogers specializes in hand-painted canvas purses, with matching skirts and hats; also features denim skirts, and bags in velvet, cotton, and wool. Prices range from $25 to $45.

Open April through December, Monday through Saturday 10 to 3; January through March, by chance or appointment. **Directions:** From Route 6 exit 9, go north on Route 134 to Setucket, then go right. At the stop sign, turn right onto Slough Road. (617) 385-2285.

Hand-painted purses by Linda Rogers, Linda's Originals, Brewster

Sheep Pond Pottery (Stonehorse Collection, Inc.), 3 Jolly's Crossing Road, 02631. Professional. Shop specializes in custom stoneware — bathroom and bar sinks, one-of-a-kind kerosene and electric lamps, dinnerware, cookware, and other functional items. Prices range from $5 to $500. Says potter Michael Garrison, "I'm hard to find, and people, once they get here, feel as though they have found something special."

Open all year, Monday through Saturday 10 to 5. **Directions:** From Route 6 exit 10, head north on Route 124 for 2 miles, to Fisherman's Landing Road. A sign for the pottery is on the left; follow arrows until you reach the shop. "Keep the faith and keep going." (617) 896-3845.

Society of Cape Cod Craftsmen Annual Fair, Brewster Community Center, Route 6A (Box 534, Harwich, 02645). A 3-day juried crafts fair beginning the second Wednesday in August. Hours: 9 to 6. Approximately 35 professional craftspeople exhibiting, selling, and demonstrating woodcarving, jewelry, leather work, metalwork, pottery, scrimshaw, and stained glass. 10,000 visitors annually. Admission free. **Directions:** From Route 6 exit 10, head north on Route 124 to Route 6A; then turn right onto Route 6A and continue ½ mile to the community center. (617) 896-3845.

The Spectrum of American Artists and Craftsmen, Inc., 369 Old King's Highway, 02631. Professional. Selections include weaving, soft sculpture, enamels, leather, paintings, sculptures, and photography. Also etchings; hand-built and hand-thrown stoneware, raku, and porcelain; sterling silver and gold jewelry with precious and semiprecious stones; blown glass; contemporary art glass; and leaded stained glass. Prices range from $1 to $2,500.

Open daily all year, summer 9:30 to 6, winter 10 to 5. **Directions:** Take Route 6 exit 9 to Route 134. Head north on Route 134 to Route 6A; then turn right and go about 1½ miles. The gallery is on the left. (617) 385-3322.

The Strawberry Patch, Route 6A (Box 689), 02631. Professional and amateur. Selections include patchwork quilts, hand-woven rugs, pillows, afghans, blankets, and fabrics; also features baby gifts, gifts for the kitchen, and holiday ornaments. Prices range from $1 to $400. All items are displayed in the original stalls and loft of a century-old horse barn.

Open May and June, daily 10 to 5; July and August, daily 9 to 9; September through November, daily 10 to 5. **Directions:** Take Route 6 exit 9 to Route 134. Follow Route 134 north to Route 6A and turn right. Go approximately 5 miles to The Strawberry Patch, which is on the right. (617) 896-5050.

BRIMFIELD

The Pistachio Potter, East Hill Road, 01010. Professional. Shop features the work of a potter-and-water-colorist team. Pottery, designed and executed on the premises by Eileen Niejadlik, includes vases, pots, cutout lanterns, lamps with dried-flower shades, and a complete line of dinnerware. Custom orders for pottery accepted. Water colorist Paul Niejadlik offers paintings of rural New England. Prices range from $2.50 to $100. The shop is in the Niejadlik home.

Open all year — "drop in anytime or call to make sure we're at home." **Directions:** Take Interstate 90 exit 9 (Sturbridge) onto Interstate 86. Head south to Route 20, about 3 miles, then follow Route 20 west to Brimfield. At the town common and traffic light, turn right, then bear right down Brookfield Road; then immediately turn right onto East Hill Road. The shop is in the fifth house on the right. (413) 245-3498.

BROCKTON

Macramé by Mike, 730 North Main Street, 02401. Amateur. Michael Bates's shop features macramé in a variety of forms — from pieces for everyday use to seasonal items. Prices range from $1 to $150.

Open all year, Tuesday 6 to 9, Wednesday and Thursday 11 to 9, Friday and Saturday 11 to 6. **Directions:** Take Route 128 to Route 24 south to Route 27. Head east on Route 27 to the first traffic light, then turn right onto Oak Street. Continue for 3 miles, then turn right onto North Main Street. The shop is about ½ mile ahead on the right. (617) 587-2972.

BROOKLINE

Marion-Ruth, 1385 Beacon Street, 02146. Professional. Shop features ceramics, studio glass, metal and wood sculpture, and weaving. Prices range from $10 to $500. There is a large display area in which complete collections of artists' works are exhibited.

Open all year, Monday through Saturday 9:30 to 5:30. **Directions:** Marion-Ruth is 2 blocks west of Coolidge Corner, on the south side of Beacon Street. (617) 734-6620.

Blown-glass vase by Chris Heilman and Joyce Roessler, Ten Arrow, Cambridge

BUZZARDS BAY

Joseph V. Zlogar, Wooden Toys, 8 Alderberry Road, 02532. Professional. Studio specializes in wooden toys. Prices range from $2.50 to $27.50. Zlogar creates all toys from native pine in his home studio, and finishes them in polyurethane for durability.

Open all year, by appointment. **Directions:** From the junction of routes 6 and 28, take Saint Margaret's Street to Puritan Road. Turn right onto Puritan Road, then right again onto Alderberry Road. (617) 759-4645.

CAMBRIDGE

The Christmas Store, various locations in town. 6-week juried crafts cooperative lasting from the second week in November through Christmas Eve. Open daily, variable hours. 75 professional and amateur craftspeople and artists exhibit ceramics, woodwork, weaving, clothing, glass, leather, and holiday ornaments. The Christmas Store, an annual crafts cooperative, is set up in a different Cambridge location each year. It is organized and staffed by the craftspeople and artists whose works are exhibited and sold in the store. Weekly demonstrations of various crafts are given. Admission free. Please call Directory Assistance for the telephone number of the store, then call the store to find out its location for the current year.

E. M. Klim Studio, 25 Antrim Street, 02139. Professional. Klim specializes in copper enameling of plates of various sizes and designs, and also does electro-formed dishes and jewelry. Prices range from $5 to $500.

Open evenings, by appointment only. **Directions:** Take Interstate 90 Cambridge exit onto River Street. Follow River Street (which becomes Prospect Street) to Broadway, and turn left onto Broadway. Antrim Street is the third street on the right. (617) 864-0362.

Friends Gallery, 383 Huron Avenue, 02138. Professional and amateur. Gallery features a wide range of fine handcrafts such as clothing for both children and adults, leather handbags, wrought iron, copperware, pewter, and rugs. Prices range from $5 to $600. Everything is "of very high quality and consistent good taste."

Open mid-September through mid-June, Tuesday through Saturday 10:30 to 4:30. **Directions:** At the end of Route 2 east, continue past the rotary toward Fresh Pond. Turn east onto Huron Avenue and go 3 blocks. The shop is set back and is marked by a sign. (617) 547-1267.

Michael Weiss, Handcrafted Furniture, 69 Harvey Street, 02140. Professional. Shop specializes in platform beds, Parsons tables, butcher-block tables, shelving, benches, and sofas; also carries Shaker peg racks, cutting boards, serving platters, spice racks, rocking horses for infants, and other small items. Prices range from $5 to $100. Pieces are noted for "quality and care in both design and execution, the careful use of mixed woods, and our willingness to do custom variations."

Open all year, Monday through Friday 9 to 6, Saturday 11 to 5. **Directions:** From Harvard Square,

To get to Cambridge, take Route 128 exit 46A onto Route 2 east. Follow Route 2 to the end, and go one third of the way around the rotary onto Route 16 (Alewife Brook Parkway). Continue to the junction with Massachusetts Avenue, and turn right. Follow Massachusetts Avenue into Harvard Square. Or, from Boston, take the subway red line to Harvard Station.

follow Massachusetts Avenue northwest for about 10 minutes, then turn left onto Harvey Street. The shop is in north Cambridge, 1 mile from the Arlington town line. (617) 661-7709.

Project Arts Center Show, 141 Huron Avenue, 02138. A 22-day juried crafts event, sponsored by the Project Arts Center and held in December. Hours: 10 to 7. Approximately 50 professional and amateur craftspeople exhibit pottery, jewelry, hand-printed cards, wooden toys, and soft sculptures. Several thousand visitors annually. Admission free. **Directions:** From Harvard Square, follow Massachusetts Avenue northwest and turn left onto Linnaean Street. At the end of the street, turn right onto Garden Street. At the top of the hill by the fire station, turn left onto Huron Avenue. The center is on the right, in the first block. (617) 491-0187.

Sundial Batik Studio, 340 Huron Avenue, 02138. Professional. Studio features original batik artwork by the artist/owner, including framed batik paintings, wall hangings, and soft sculptures. The gallery/studio also has a large selection of other batik items such as clothing from the Philippines, Singapore, and India. Prices range from $5 to $200. This is a working studio where visitors can watch the batik process from design concept through execution in waxes and dyes.

Open all year, Monday through Friday 10:30 to 6, Saturday 11 to 5; month of December, also open Thursday evening and Sunday — call for hours. **Directions:** From Harvard Square, follow Massachusetts Avenue northwest and turn left onto Linnaean Street, then right onto Garden Street. Follow to the traffic light at the intersection with Huron Avenue, and turn left. Go about 8 blocks. Sundial is on the left. (617) 864-2660.

Ten Arrow Gallery/Shop, 10 Arrow Street, 02138. Professional. Selections include sculptural furniture, wooden boxes, blown glass, both one-of-a-kind and production ceramics and jewelry, cast-bronze and ceramic bells, and wrought iron. Prices range from $1 to $4,000. This is a comprehensive gallery and shop selling works in all media in a wide range of prices.

Open all year, Monday through Saturday 10 to 6, plus open Thursday to 9. **Directions:** From Harvard Square, follow Massachusetts Avenue southeast to Arrow Street, and turn right. (617) 876-1117.

Eighteenth-century whaler engraved on sperm-whale tooth by Marcy Pumphret, Scrimshaw by Marcy at Grasshopper Acres, Chatham

CENTERVILLE

Roy L. Dupuy, Ship Carving, 1301 Bumps River Road, 02632. Professional. Dupuy offers wood items carved in his home workshop — eagles, pineapples, whales, and other figures; also weather vanes, quarterboards, and other signs. Pieces cost $30 to $350 and up.

Open by appointment only. (617) 775-2215.

CHATHAM

Chatham Festival of the Arts, Chase Park, Cross Street. 3-day juried crafts festival, sponsored by the Creative Arts Center of Chatham (Box 368, 02633) and held the third weekend of August. Hours: 10 to 5. Approximately 100 professional and amateur craftspeople and artists exhibit stained glass, blown glass, woodwork, weaving, soft sculpture, jewelry, bird carvings, and pottery. Demonstrations of some crafts. 5,000 visitors annually. Admission free. **Directions:** Chase Park is in the center of Chatham village. (617) 945-3583.

Fletcher III, Handcrafted Pewter, 255 Old Harbor Road, 02633. Professional. Shop specializes in pewter jewelry in shell designs. Hollowware designed by a husband-and-wife team is also sold. Prices range from $8.50 to $200.

Open all year, Monday through Saturday 9 to 5. **Directions:** As you approach Chatham from Route 28, the shop is about ½ mile beyond the rotary, in a private residence on the left. (617) 945-3441.

Old Scrimshaw Leather Shop, 616 Main Street, 02633. Professional. Shop features a wide variety of leather goods including handbags, wallets, belts, briefcases, sandals, vests, jackets, and boots. Prices range from $2 to $200. The decor of the shop is unique — "barn board, burlap, and antiques." Many goods are made on the premises.

Open January through May, Monday through Saturday 10 to 5:30; June through August, Monday through Saturday 10 to 10, Sunday from 11; September through December, Monday through Saturday 10 to 5:30, Sunday from 11. **Directions:** Old Scrimshaw is located in downtown Chatham. (617) 945-1911.

Scrimshaw by Marcy at Grasshopper Acres, 333 Old Harbor Road, 02633. Professional. Marcy Pumphret offers her own engraved whale ivory and jewelry for both men and women. She also carries nautical antiques and American Eskimo carvings. Prices range from $13 to $400. Pumphret sells from her working studio, gives engraving demonstrations, and provides materials and books to browse through.

Open all year, by chance and appointment. **Directions:** The studio is about ¾ mile beyond the Route 28 rotary, on the left, in a white house marked by a large white anchor. (617) 945-0782.

Thomas Odell Jewelry, 423 Main Street, 02633. Professional. Thomas Odell offers jewelry in 14- and 18-karat gold and in sterling silver, using a wide range of metal-forming techniques and precious and semiprecious stones. The shop also carries sculptured pieces in bronze, brass, copper, stainless steel, and mild steel. Prices range from $10 to $1,500. All work is created in a

To get to Chatham, take Route 6 east exit 11 to Route 137. Take Route 137 south to Route 28 (Old Harbor Road). Turn left onto Route 28 and continue about 5½ miles, staying on Route 28 around the rotary, to Chatham village.

workshop on the premises.

Open June through December, Tuesday through Saturday 10 to 5; January through May, Thursday through Saturday 10 to 5. **Directions:** From the Route 28 rotary, turn onto Main Street, then go ½ mile east to the shop. (617) 945-3239.

CHESTERFIELD

Seth Isman Pottery, South Street (Box 167), 01012. Professional. Studio features functional stoneware pottery, with dinnerware a specialty. Also sold are mixing-bowl sets, canister sets, pie plates, and cookie jars. Prices range from $7 to $90. Isman pays careful attention to the functions of the pieces he makes, incorporating "elegant designs and cheerful colors" into them. A free color brochure is available.

Open all year, daily 10 to 5. Visitors welcome, but please call ahead. **Directions:** Take Interstate 91 to Northampton, then Route 9 west about 10 miles to Williamsburg. Then follow Route 143 west about 6 miles to Chesterfield. Call for specific directions to the pottery. (413) 296-4729.

To get to Cohasset, take Route 3 exit 30 (Hingham) onto Route 228, and follow signs to Cohasset.

COHASSET

U.S. Bells, 300 South Main Street, 02025. Professional. This private studio specializes in copper-plate and steel wind bells, fashioned by craftsman Robert C. Kingsland. Prices range from $20 to $60. Kingsland is one of "only three or four makers of wind bells in the country."

Open by appointment only. (617) 383-9344.

The Wee Spinnaker, 11 Elm Street (4 Stagecoach Way), 02025. Professional and amateur. Shop features crib toys, cradles, soft sculptures, pillows, Beatrix Potter lamps and mirrors, dolls, doll houses, stuffed animals, and herb wreaths. Prices range from $1 to $175. Over four hundred people from all over the country "make unusual items of very fine quality" for The Wee Spinnaker.

Open all year, Monday through Saturday 10 to 5, Sunday from 1. **Directions:** At the junction of routes 228 and 3A turn right onto Route 3A and continue about 1 mile to the flashing yellow light. Then turn left onto Sohier Street, and follow it to the end. Turn right, then turn left in the center of town by Cohasset Hardware. The shop is the first on the right. (617) 383-6395.

CONCORD

The Catseye, Independence Court, 01742. Professional. Shop specializes in crafts in wood, glass, and fiber; also carries gold and silver jewelry. Jewelry repair and restoration done. Prices range from $10 to $1,000.

Open all year, Tuesday through Saturday 9 to 5. **Directions:** Take Route 128 to Route 2 west, then follow signs about 5 miles to town. The shop is downtown, just off Main Street. (617) 369-8377.

DEERFIELD

Old Deerfield Summer and Fall Craft Fairs, Memorial Hall Museum, 01342. A pair of 2-day juried crafts fairs, sponsored by Memorial Hall Museum and held the last weekend of June and the last weekend of September. Summer hours: 10 to 5. Fall hours: 10 to 4. At each fair, 125 professional craftspeople exhibit a wide variety of crafts, with an emphasis on early American crafts. 10,000 visitors to each show annually. Admission free. **Directions:** Heading north on Interstate 91, take exit 24, then go north on Route 5 for 6 miles to town. (413) 773-8929, or 773-5206.

DENNIS

Eden Hand Arts, intersection of Dr. Lord's Road, Route 6A, and Sesuit Neck Road (Box 585), 02638. Professional. Shop offers Eve Carey's pottery (wheel-thrown majolica ware fired at high temperatures), with an emphasis on decorative lamps. Also available here is John Carey's gold and sterling silver jewelry. Prices range from $5 to $600. "We are a small, intimate gallery, preferring one-to-one relationships with customers."

Open July through Labor Day, Monday through Saturday 10 to 5. **Directions:** Take Route 6A to Dr. Lord's and Sesuit Neck roads. (617) 385-9708.

Hesperus Pottery and Artisans Co-op, Nobscusset Settlement (Pleasant Bay Road, Harwich, 02645). Professional. Shop features folk-art paintings, country stoneware, quilts, woodcuts, water colors, soft sculptures, and antiques. Prices range from $5 to $60. "The shop is a joint effort of seven women — Cape Cod natives and those who have chosen life here because of its tranquil lifestyle, conducive to the pursuit of art."

Open June through Labor Day, daily 10 to 5; September to Christmas, weekends 10 to 5. **Directions:** Heading east into Dennis on Route 6A, you'll find Nobscusset Settlement on the right. The co-op is in this group of stores. (617) 432-3704.

Randy and Elaine Fisher, Bird Carvings, 5 Walden Place, 02638. Professional. The Fishers specialize in birds hand carved from basswood, painted in acrylics, and mounted on natural driftwood bases; some are depicted in natural settings. Prices range from $50 to $2,000. Both Fishers are avid bird watchers and amateur ornithologists who "spend some time during the spring and fall migrations banding and researching birds to

Majolica lamp and cut-out shade by John and Eve Carey, Eden Hand Arts, Dennis

To get to Dennis, take Route 6 exit 8. Head north, then turn right onto Route 6A.

77

Candle castle by Gail Turner, Mill Stone Pottery, East Dennis

help make our carvings more realistic."

Open all year, by appointment only. **Directions:** From Route 6A, turn south onto South Yarmouth Road. Go ¼ mile, then turn left onto Thoreau Drive. Turn left onto SouWest Drive, then left again onto Walden Place. The shop is on the corner of SouWest Drive and Walden Place. (617) 385-2880.

DORCHESTER

Jean Goldman Clay Sculpture, 36 Van Winkle Street, 02124. Professional. Shop features one-of-a-kind clay sculptures of animals and people, from two inches tall to garden sized. Pieces are crafted of high-fired materials, with figures reminiscent of pre-Columbian and ancient oriental animals and people. Prices range from $5 to $400. Goldman's sculptures reflect whimsy and humor, and express many moods.

Open all year, by appointment only. (617) 436-1830.

DUNSTABLE

Federal Furnace Pottery, Inc., Hardy Street, 01827. Professional. Shop specializes in one-of-a-kind pieces in porcelain, stoneware, and raku. Selections include sculptural and functional pieces, and also drawings and lithographs. Prices range from $5 to $2,000. The pottery is made on the premises, in the artists' studios.

Open all year, daily 10 to 6. **Directions:** Take Route 128 to Route 3 north (Nashua, NH). Exit onto Route 113 and head toward Dunstable, following the red-and-white signs for the pottery. (617) 649-7402.

DUXBURY

Mariposa, 35 Depot Street (Box 1590), 02332. Professional and amateur. Selections include pottery, blown glass, baskets, stenciled mirrors, toys, water colors, woodcuts, mobiles, jewelry, paperweights, and potpourri. Prices begin at $10. Mariposa features a large inventory and an "inventive mix" of merchandise.

Open all year, Monday through Saturday 9:30 to 5:30, Sunday 1 to 5. **Directions:** Heading south from Boston on Route 3, take exit 33 and turn right onto Route 14. Go 1 mile to traffic light, and then turn right onto Route 3A. Go 1 mile more, and turn left onto Depot Street. The shop is one of the Duxbury Crossroads shops. (617) 934-6961.

To get to East Dennis, take Route 6A through Dennis to East Dennis.

EAST DENNIS

Mill Stone Pottery, South Street, 02641. Professional. Shop features both functional and decorative pottery —

items such as castle candle holders, bird feeders, tile lazy Susans, wall plaques, and mirrors. Prices range from $3 to $200. Pottery is glazed using wax (batik) methods. The shop is housed in an old windmill.

Open mid-June through August, Monday through Saturday 10 to 5; September to mid-June, Wednesday through Friday noon to 5, Saturday from 10. **Directions:** From Route 6A in East Dennis, turn onto South Street and follow the signs. (617) 255-6140.

Ol' Salty's Quarterboards, 28 J.H. Sears Road (Box 45), 02641. Professional. Henry H. Sears makes mahogany quarterboards in many designs and sizes. Prices range from $15 to $65.

Open all year, Monday through Saturday 9 to 4. **Directions:** From Route 6A, take School Street to J.H. Sears Road, near the Dennis/Brewster town line. The shop is near Sesuit Harbor, "way off the beaten path." (617) 385-3143.

EAST LONGMEADOW

Yankee Heritage Gift Shoppe, 205 North Main Street, 01028. Professional. Shop features early-American country painting by Jo Gobeille on old and antique wood and tinware. Also sells original handmade dolls, porcelain, and scrimshaw. Prices range from $5 to $150. "We search constantly for the finest craftspeople and artists who have something uniquely their own to offer. We feature the 'unusual' artisan."

Open January to Thanksgiving, Monday through Saturday 10 to 5; day after Thanksgiving through December, same hours plus open Thursday to 8, and, for 1 week before Christmas, evenings to 8. **Directions:** Heading north on Interstate 91, take exit 2 and follow routes 83 and 21 to Sumner Avenue. Take a right onto Sumner Avenue (which is still routes 83 and 21) and follow to East Longmeadow. The shop is about 3½ miles ahead at Four Corners traffic light, across from Willow Glen Restaurant. (413) 525-2363.

EAST SANDWICH

Heather House, 350 Route 6A (Box 321), 02537. Professional and amateur. Selections include sewn, quilted, and patchwork goods such as pillows, wreaths, aprons, fabric baskets and frames, and desk accessories. There is a children's corner displaying handmade dolls, quilts, sweaters, bibs, stuffed animals, and wood and fabric toys. Prices range from $1 to $300. "Everything at Heather House is of excellent quality and in good taste, with a wide range of prices to fit anyone's pocketbook....No junk!"

Open January 15 through March, Wednesday

To get to East Sandwich, take Route 6 exit 3 onto Quaker Meeting House Road to Route 6A.

through Sunday 10 to 5; April and May, Tuesday through Sunday 10 to 5; June through December, daily 10 to 6. **Directions:** From the Quaker Meeting House Road, turn right onto Route 6A. The shop is in the second building on the right. (617) 888-2034.

The Paper Silk Moon, 15 Foster Road (RD 1), 02537. Professional. Shop specializes in hand-silk-screened cards, place mats, napkins, wall hangings, skirts, caftans, and fine-art prints. Prices range from $2 to $100. All items are original designs.

Open by appointment only. (617) 888-5124.

EDGARTOWN

The Handworks, Winter Street (Box 371), 02539. Professional. Selections include the shop's own hand-woven wool and mohair scarves, stoles, and blankets. Also featured are a large variety of stoneware and porcelain pottery, stuffed animals, puppets, dolls, and leather wallets and folios. Prices range from $1 to $150. The Handworks is "a unique combination of hard-to-find items and reasonable prices."

Open June through August, daily 10 to 10; September through May, Monday through Saturday 10 to 5. **Directions:** Take the ferry from Woods Hole, Falmouth, or Hyannis to Martha's Vineyard, and follow signs to Edgartown. From Main Street, take the first left onto North Water Street, and the next left onto Winter Street. The shop is the second store from the corner. (617) 627-8402.

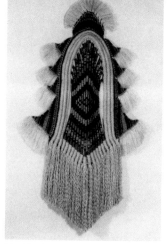

Wall hanging by Carolyn Bell, Fiber Sculpture, Great Barrington

FOXBOROUGH

The Green Onion, 7 East Street, 02035. Professional. Shop features pottery, patchwork, stained glass, and jewelry, with many pieces one of a kind. Items cost $5 to $100 and up. Emphasizes high-quality workmanship and a large variety of unusual and functional merchandise.

Open June through August, Thursday through Saturday 10 to 5; September through May, Tuesday through Saturday 10 to 5, Sunday from noon. **Directions:** Take Interstate 95 to Foxborough center, then follow Cocasset Street 3 miles. Go left under the railroad trestle onto East Street. The shop is ½ mile ahead on the right. (617) 543-2293.

GRAFTON

The Weed Lady, Moroney Road, 01519. Professional and amateur. Shop specializes in dried flowers and herbs in sachets, wreaths, and arrangements. Also sells hand-thrown pottery, miniature tin weather vanes, and carved sea birds. Prices range from $1 to $200. A wide range of items is displayed in a unique country-barn shop in an unspoiled setting.

Open August through May, Saturday and Sunday noon to 5; June and July by chance. **Directions:** Take Interstate 90 exit 11 onto Route 122. Follow Route 122 east to Route 140, and head south on Route 140 to Grafton. Moroney Road is off Route 140. (617) 839-6563.

GREAT BARRINGTON

To get to Great Barrington, take Route 7 or Route 23.

Carolyn Bell, Fiber Sculpture, 111 West Avenue (Box 134), 01230. Professional. Studio specializes in unique fiber sculptures, such as wall hangings, for both residential and commercial interiors. Bell's wall hangings are dimensional, highly textured, and original in design. Prices range from $70 to $2,000.

Open all year, Monday through Friday 9 to 5, weekends by appointment. **Directions:** Take Route 7 or Route 23 to town. (413) 528-1608.

Southern Berkshire Leather Works, 9 Railroad Street, 01230. Professional. Shop features leather work in many forms, especially notebook covers, briefcases, belts, and book covers. Prices range from $10 to $150.

Open all year, Monday through Saturday 9 to 5. **Directions:** Heading north through the town's business district, take the second left after the police station; as you are heading south, Railroad Street is the second street on the right after the post office. (413) 528-4884.

Wonderful Things, 232 Stockbridge Road, 01230. Professional and amateur. Six shops sell finished crafts in many media, including items in silver, stoneware, glass, and weaving. There are fourteen display rooms of crafts and materials. Prices range from 1¢ to $18,000.

Open all year, Monday through Saturday 10 to 5, Sunday from 1 (except closed Wednesday, January through June). **Directions:** At the junction of routes 7 and 23, head north on Route 7 for ½ mile. The shop is next to Friendly's Ice Cream. (413) 578-2473.

HADLEY

Skera, 123 Russell Street, 01035. Professional. Shop features American crafts — mostly from New England — such as ceramics, metalwork, jewelry, glass, weaving, wood, batik, and leather work. Prices range from $2 to $2,000.

Open all year, Saturday through Wednesday 11 to 6, Thursday and Friday to 9. **Directions:** Heading north on Interstate 91, take exit 19 onto Route 9. Go 2 miles to the large yellow house on the right, which is the shop. (413) 586-4563.

Stoneware bird feeder, Dorie Weintraub/Crow Point Pottery, Hingham

HINGHAM

Dorie Weintraub/Crow Point Pottery, 33 Jarvis Avenue, 02043. Professional. Studio features porcelain Christmas ornaments, stoneware decorated with Chinese brushwork, thrown stoneware, and porcelain castles. Pieces cost $1.25 to $100 and up. Weintraub creates Christmas ornaments that are "very popular and different, with a European quality" about them.

Open most of the year, Monday through Friday 9 to 3:30, but "somewhat less in summer — nice beach down the street!" Visitors welcome by appointment. (617) 749-3869.

HOLLISTON

Heritage Artisans, Inc., 400 Washington Street, 01746. Professional and amateur. Selections include stained glass, toys, baby items, dried arrangements, silver jewelry, hand-knit and crocheted items, and pottery. Special orders accepted. Prices range from 50¢ to $100.

Open all year, Monday through Saturday 10 to 5; plus month of December, Sunday from 1. **Directions:** From Interstate 495, exit onto Route 126. Heritage Artisans is located in the Wilding Building, at the junction of routes 126 and 16. (617) 429-2559.

HYANNIS

The Spectrum of American Artists and Craftsmen, Inc., 433 Main Street (369 Old King's Highway, Brewster, 02631). Selections include weaving, soft sculptures, enamels, leather, paintings, sculptures, and photography. Also etchings; hand-built and hand-thrown stoneware, raku, and porcelain; sterling silver and gold jewelry with precious and semiprecious stones; blown glass; contemporary art glass; and leaded stained glass. Prices range from $1 to $2,500.

Open daily all year, summer 9:30 AM to 10 PM, winter 10 to 5:30. **Directions:** Take Route 6 exit 6 onto Route 132, and follow Route 132 to the airport rotary. Then turn right onto Barnstable Road, and follow to Main Street. Turn right onto Main Street; the gallery is next to Meyers Furniture. (617) 771-4554.

LENOX

Weavings by Katharine Pincus, Under Mountain Road, 01240. Professional. Pincus offers hand-woven scarves, shawls, window shades, and table linens. Prices range from $15 to $400.

Open all year, by appointment only. (413) 637-1289.

LEVERETT

Leverett Craftsmen and Artists' Annual Fall Show, Montague Road, 01054. A 5-week crafts event, sponsored by Leverett Craftsmen and Artists, Inc. and held during the foliage season of October and November. Hours: daily noon to 5. About 35 professional craftspeople exhibit soft sculpture, ethnic clothing, ceramics, blown glass, wooden ware, macramé, photography, and prints. Admission free. (413) 549-6871.

Leverett Craftsmen and Artists, Inc., Montague Road, 01054. Professional. Selections include a wide variety of ceramics, porcelain, stoneware, woven pillows and clothing, jewelry, stained and blown glass, etchings and lithographs, wood furniture, and other household items in wood. Prices begin at $5, and average $20 to $60. Artists' studios are on the premises.
Open all year, daily noon to 5. (413) 549-6871.

To get to Leverett, take Interstate 91 exit 19, then take Route 9 east to Amherst. From Amherst take Route 63 north about 5 miles, then turn right onto Depot Road. Follow signs about 2 miles to Leverett Center.

LUNENBURG

To get to Lunenburg, take Route 2A from Route 2.

The Buttonwood Shop, 1 Main Street, 01462. Professional and amateur. Shop features a wide variety of crafts, the products of twenty potters and eight fiber craftspeople. Other pieces include stained glass, blown glass, paintings, prints, leather work, batik, jewelry, and wool goods. Prices range from $2 to $100.
Open January through June, Tuesday through Saturday 10 to 5; July and August, Wednesday through Friday 10 to 5; September through November, Tuesday through Saturday 10 to 5; month of December, Monday through Saturday 10 to 5. **Directions:** The shop is in the village, behind the post office. (617) 582-6706.

Lunenburg Arts Festival, elementary school grounds, Route 2A. A 1-day event, sponsored by the Lunenburg Center for Arts and Crafts (Box 433, 01462) and held the first Saturday in May. Hours: 10 to 5. About 100 professional and amateur craftspeople exhibit pottery, fiber, woodwork, paintings, prints, photography, leather work, and stained glass. Demonstrations of spinning, weaving, and pottery. Food available. 1,000 visitors annually. Admission free. (617) 582-4041.

Turkey Hill Studio, 40 Rolling Acres Road, 01462. Professional. Studio specializes in Russ and Pauline Coburn's carvings of songbirds, shore birds, upland game birds, and birds of prey. Prices range from $65 to $3,000. The Coburns emphasize "our personal technique."
Open all year, by appointment only. (617) 582-6306.

MARBLEHEAD

Quaigh Design Centre, Chandlers Row, Spring and

Pleasant streets, 01945. Professional. Selections include stained glass, stoneware and porcelain pottery, sterling silver and gold jewelry, woven lamps and shades, and handmade cards. Prices range from $2 to $350. "The high quality of our crafts has been the reason our customers have come back year after year."

Open May through December, Monday through Saturday 10 to 5:30, Sunday 1 to 5; January through April, Monday through Saturday 10 to 5:30. **Directions:** Take Route 128 to Route 114, and follow Route 114 to town. Quaigh Design Centre is in the center of town. (617) 631-4016.

"Cobblestone Road" by Rebecca Levine, Tactile Artist, Nantucket

MASHPEE

Splinter Designs, Pondview Avenue (Box 411), 02649. Professional. Shop specializes in hardwood furniture and offers other hardwood domestic accessories in original designs. Prices range from $5 to $600. "Our style features gentle curves, clean lines, and hand-planed surfaces with natural finishes. Sandpaper is seldom used, since hand tools leave wood glass smooth."

Open all year, Monday through Saturday 9 to 5. **Directions:** Head south on Route 28, and exit onto Route 151. Go toward Mashpee and, after 5 miles, turn left onto Algonquin Avenue, toward Johns Pond. Pondview Avenue is the first right after the pond. (617) 477-9909.

MIDDLEBOROUGH

Pulsifer Family Pottery, 376 Plymouth Street, 02346. Professional. The Pulsifers specialize in functional porcelain and stoneware, and also offer luster-glazed pieces. Prices range from $10 to $100. The pottery shop and gallery are in a family setting; works are on display in the studio and throughout the home.

Open all year, Saturday and Sunday 10 to 7. **Directions:** Take Route 128 to Route 24. Head south on Route 24 (which becomes Route 25) about 20 miles to Route 44. Follow Route 44 east to the third traffic light; turn left, and go 1 mile to the studio, which is in a house on the right. (617) 947-8613.

MILTON

Ceramic Cellar and Gallery, 31 Brush Hill Lane, 02186. Professional. The gallery features high-fired stoneware vases, planters, trays, bowls, wall collages, pocket planters for walls, and tiles. Prices range from $5 to $120. Each piece is one of a kind.

Open all year, by appointment only. (617) 333-0367.

NANTUCKET

Artisans Cooperative, 60 Main Street (Box 216, Chadds Ford, PA 19317). Professional. Selections include traditional handmade quilts, one-of-a-kind clothing designs, hand-woven blankets and tapestries, functional and decorative stained glass, metalwork, wood, and baskets. Prices range from $2 to $700. Artisans Cooperative is a non-profit organization providing work and experience for rural craftspeople through the production of hand-crafted items.

To get to Nantucket, take the ferry from either Woods Hole or Hyannis.

Open April through December, daily 9 to 5. **Directions:** Main Street is in the heart of Nantucket village. (617) 228-4631.

Bobbi Wade's Clothing, Easton Street, 02554. Professional. Shop specializes in original-design clothing, especially shirts and coordinates. Prices range from $23 to $80. Designs are similar to those of workshirts worn in the 1800s.

Open June through September, daily 9 to 9; October through December, and March through May, by chance; please call ahead. (617) 228-9334.

The Lion's Paw, Zero Main Street, 02554. Professional and amateur. Shop offers antique, imported, and "lightship" baskets; porcelain and stoneware hand crafted throughout America and Europe; rugs from Poland, Ethiopia, India, and Morocco; gold and silver jewelry; and glassware. Also, primitive water colors and carvings. Prices range from $1 to $1,000.

Open month of April, weekends 10 to 5; May and June, daily 9 to 6; July through Labor Day, daily 9 AM to 9:30 PM; day after Labor Day through December, daily 9 to 6. **Directions:** The shop is at the end of Main Street, in the red building. (617) 228-3837.

Nantucket Looms, 16 Main Street, 02554. Professional. Shop specializes in hand-woven goods such as mohair and wool blankets, stoles, and ascots. Also sold are tweeds, upholstery fabrics, wall coverings, and rugs. Custom orders accepted. Prices range from $15 to $150. Weavers use natural fibers only.

Open July and August, Monday through Saturday 10 to 5; September through June, Tuesday through Saturday 10 to 5. (617) 228-1908.

R. Levine, Tactile Artist, "Canton" Still Dock, 02554. Professional. Rebecca Levine offers small tapestries that average 9 by 14 inches in size. Levine has termed them "tactiles" because they incorporate areas of sculpturally cut pile of various yarn types (including silks), and therefore offer different textures to the viewer to touch and investigate. She produces a limited number of these each year, mainly for sale in galleries, but welcomes visitors. Prices begin at $175.

Open all year, by appointment only. (617) 228-1938.

The Spectrum of American Artists and Craftsmen, Inc., 26 Main Street (369 Old King's Highway, Brewster, 02631). Professional. Selections include weaving, soft sculpture, enamels, leather, paintings, sculptures, and photography. Also etchings; hand-built and hand-thrown stoneware, raku, and porcelain; sterling silver and gold jewelry with precious and semi-precious stones; blown glass; contemporary art glass; and leaded stained glass. Prices range from $1 to $2,500.

Open mid-April to Christmas, 9:30 AM to 10 PM; winter hours may vary — call for verification. (617) 385-3322.

The Wee Spinnaker, 29 Centre Street, 02554. Professional and amateur. Shop features soft sculptures, pillows, Beatrix Potter lamps and mirrors, dolls, doll houses, stuffed animals, carved birds, and herb wreaths. Prices range from $1 to $175. Over four hundred people from all over the country "make unusual items of very fine quality" for The Wee Spinnaker.

Open mid-May through June, daily 10 to 5; July through Labor Day, daily 10 to 10; day after Labor Day through mid-October, daily 10 to 5. **Directions:** The shop is part of the Meeting House Collection.

NEW BEDFORD

Thomas Clemmey Stained Glass Studio, 206 Whitman Street, 02745. Professional. Clemmey creates stained-glass pieces such as free-standing sculptures, windows, door panels, wall hangings, lamps, and sun catchers. Prices range from $2 to $1,400.

Open during school year, Monday through Friday 3 to 11, weekends and holidays from 8 AM; summer months, daily 8 AM to 11 PM. **Directions:** Take Interstate 195 to Washburn or Coggeshall Street exit. The studio is 1½ miles north of the exit. (617) 996-1418.

To get to Newburyport, take Interstate 95 to Route 113 east. Or, take Route 495 to Route 110 east.

NEWBURYPORT

Federal Street Lighthouse, Ltd., 38 Market Square, 01950. Professional. Shop specializes in handmade reproductions of traditional lighting devices — sconces, chandeliers, and lanterns. Also carries Japan-lacquer fire screens, mirrors, reproduction ironware, and etched-glass lamp shades. Prices range from $20 to $600. "Great attention is paid to selling correct and period reproductions for the serious restorer."

Open all year, Tuesday through Saturday 10:30 to 5, Sunday from 1. **Directions:** The shop is downtown, in the restored waterfront Market Square area, across from the old fire station. (617) 462-6333.

Piel Craftsmen, 307 High Street, 01950. Professional and amateur. Shop specializes in hand-crafted ship models and miniatures of famous ships of the 1800s, such as the *Constitution,* the *Flying Cloud,* and the *Charles W. Morgan.* Each reproduction is completely assembled and finished. Prices range from $35 to $295. "As far as we know, we are the only shop of this kind."

Open all year, Monday through Friday 9 to 4. **Directions:** The shop is on Route 113, the main residential street in the town. (617) 462-7012.

Soft Pictures, 78 State Street, 01950. Professional and amateur. Shop offers sportswear for women and children, plus belts, tote bags, place mats, pillows, aprons, and skirts. Almost everything is made on the premises, and much of it is decorated. Prices range from $15 to $35. Appliqué soft wares are a specialty, as well as embroidery and other types of decorative soft pictures.

Open all year, Tuesday through Saturday 9 to 5. **Directions:** The shop is in the center of town. (617) 465-3430.

"Topaz," ship model, Piel Craftsmen, Newburyport

NEWTON

Janis Lavine, Ceramic Artist, 34 Lincoln Street, 02161. Professional. Studio specializes in fiber-slip sculpture and raku stoneware. Prices range from $10 to $150. Fiber slip is an unusual type of sculpture in which few ceramic artists work. The shop's large raku wall pieces are used by interior designers.

Open all year, Monday through Friday 9 AM to 9:30 PM; Saturday and Sunday, 9 AM to varying closing times. **Directions:** Take the Newton Highlands exit off Route 9. Turn right onto Centre Street, then left onto Walnut Street and left again onto Lincoln Street. (617) 965-3959.

Springfest, Newton City Hall grounds, 1000 Commonwealth Avenue. 1-day crafts festival, sponsored by Newton Cultural Affairs Commission (c/o Voni Weaver, 81 Neshobe Road, 02168) and held the third Sunday in May. Hours: 10 to 4. About 100 professional and amateur craftspeople exhibit ceramics, fiber work, wood, jewelry, stained glass, clothing, and leather. Some crafts are demonstrated. Food available. 3,000 to 5,000 visitors annually. Admission free. **Directions:** Take Commonwealth Avenue (Route 30) to Walnut Street. The city hall is on the corner. (617) 332-8092.

Vincent Ferrini, Designer, 141 Wood End Road, 02161. Professional. Ferrini offers one-of-a-kind custom-designed pieces in fine jewelry, hollowware, and sculpture. Prices begin at $50.

Open all year, by appointment only. (617) 527-0080.

To get to Newton, Newton Centre, Newton Highlands, and Newtonville, take Route 128 exit 55 to Route 9. Or, to reach Commonwealth Avenue, take Route 128 exit 51.

NEWTON CENTRE

Jubilation, 91 Union Street, 02159. Professional. Shop features an extensive assortment of soft sculptures, such as "basket cases" (soft, whimsical characters made from stockings). Also carries contemporary quilts, handmade paper items, leather goods, woodwork, and blown glass. Prices range from $3 to $3,000. Jubilation houses a large collection of contemporary American crafts. "Browse and enjoy as one would in a museum."

Open all year, Monday through Saturday 10 to 5. **Directions:** Take Route 9 east over the Parker Street bridge to Newton Centre. The shop is directly across from an MBTA stop. (617) 965-0488.

Soft sculpture by Jamie Menczer Greenebaum, Jubilation, Newton Centre

NEWTON HIGHLANDS

Limited Editions, Inc., 1176 Walnut Street, 02161. Professional. Shop features blown-glass candles by Brian Maytum, porcelain coat hooks and soap and toothbrush holders by Bohn Buechner, and stained-glass letter and card holders by Edie Tal — plus jewelry, quilts, toys, clothing, and accessories. Prices range from $1 to $450.

Open all year, Monday through Saturday 10 to 5:30, plus Thursday to 8; also open Thanksgiving to Christmas, Sunday noon to 5. **Directions:** Located at junction of Walnut and Lincoln streets. (617) 965-5474.

The Potters Shop, 34 Lincoln Street, 02161. Professional. Shop specializes in pottery, both functional and decorative, in many styles. Exhibits change often. Prices range from $2 to $300. All work sold is made by potters in their studios on the premises. "Visitors are welcome to visit the studios as well as the gallery."

Open all year, Monday through Friday 9 AM to 9:30 PM, Saturday 9 to 5, Sunday 11 to 5. **Directions:** Take Route 9 to Hartford Street, and go 1 block to Lincoln Street. The shop is on the corner of Hartford and Lincoln streets. (617) 965-3959.

NEWTONVILLE

The Craft Show Shop, 809 Washington Street, 02160. Professional and amateur. Selections include hand-built stoneware and other pottery, hanging planters, and jewelry. Prices range from $1 to $275. The shop houses "a tremendous variety of merchandise."

Open May through Thanksgiving, Tuesday through Saturday 11 to 5; daily Thanksgiving through Christmas. **Directions:** From Route 128, take Route 16 (Washington Street) east to the shop. From Boston, take Interstate 90 west exit 17; at the end of the ramp, go straight onto Washington Street. The shop is 1 mile ahead, on the right. (617) 965-3521.

NORTH ADAMS

The Corner/Northern Berkshire Council of the Arts, 19 Holden Street, Berkshire Plaza, 01247. Professional. Shop features combination wood cutting boards, wooden toys, children's furniture, stained and etched glass, candles made from original molds of American pressed glass, quilts, and pillows. Prices range from 50¢ to $250. All items are produced on consignment, and all are handmade in New England.

Open all year, Monday through Saturday 9 to 5. **Directions:** Park your car on Main Street, cross Main Street to the north side, and walk through the walkway behind the Berkshire Bank. The shop is directly ahead in the Berkshire Plaza, next to Peebles Jewelry Store. (413) 663-3651.

Textile Studios at Hoosuck, The Wall-Streeter, 26 Union Street (Box 1002, Williamstown, 01267). Professional. Studios specialize in yarns hand spun on the premises from natural fibers, and dyed in eighty-eight different colors. Also carries hand-woven fabrics, embroideries, mesh work, tapestries, lace work, decorator fabrics, and clothing.

Open all year, Monday through Friday 8 to 4. **Directions:** The studios are on Route 2. (413) 664-4992.

To get to North Adams, take Interstate 91 exit 26 onto Route 2. Follow Route 2 (Mohawk Trail) to the center of town.

NORTHAMPTON

Diane H. Smith Studio, 11 Walnut Street, 01060. Professional. Shop specializes in stained-glass windows created from many materials, from traditional objects to objects found in nature, such as sea shells, sea glass, and stones. Also featured are three-dimensional items: planters, boxes, and candle chimneys. Prices range from $5 to $500. Only original designs are used.

Open by appointment only. (413) 586-4009.

NORTH DARTMOUTH

Surprise Package Craftiques, 405 Old Westport Road, 02747. Professional. Shop offers women's apparel and accessories hand painted in original designs. Also carries scrimshaw jewelry and buttons, pottery, shell crafts, oil and acrylic paintings, tole products, and handmade dolls and toys. Prices range from $8 to $250. "This is the only shop of its kind in the area, and it is known for quality and unique crafts."

Open January and February, Thursday through Sunday 11 to 4; March through October, Wednesday through Sunday 11 to 4; November and December,

Tuesday through Sunday 11 to 4. **Directions:** Take Route 128 to Route 24 south to Interstate 195 east. Take exit 12 from Interstate 195, then turn right at the end of the ramp, and right again at the first traffic light (Route 6). Follow Route 6 west to the third traffic light, then turn left onto Cross Road. Follow it to the end and turn right onto Old Westport Road. The shop is ½ mile ahead, on the left, just beyond Southeastern Massachusetts University. (617) 993-8385.

To get to North Eastham, take Route 6.

NORTH EASTHAM

Billingsgate Glass, North Sunken Meadow Road (Box 429), 02651. Professional. Shop specializes in stained glass, especially reproductions of ships and sailboats in historical and contemporary motifs. There are thirty-five designs to choose from. Custom work accepted. Pieces cost $20 to $200 and up. Owner/craftsperson Suzanne Boardman works in original designs and uses the finest materials available. She incorporates classical lines and authentic rigging into her creations.

Open all year, by appointment only. (617) 255-6053.

The Glass Eye, Route 6 and Brackett Road, 02651. Professional. Shop emphasizes stained glass in the form of windows, lamps, limited-edition series, and sun catchers. Also sells stoneware, porcelain, silver and gold jewelry, blown glass, woodcarvings, and soft sculptures. Prices range from 95¢ to $1,000. Stresses the "tasteful selection of fine handcrafts from artisans throughout the Northeast."

Open January through April, Tuesday through Saturday 9 to 5; May and June, daily 9 to 5; July and August, daily 9 to 9; September to Christmas, daily 9 to 5. **Directions:** The shop is 5 miles from the Orleans rotary, in the Village Shopping Center at the traffic light. (617) 255-5044.

Serendipity Studio/Gallery, Massasoit Road (Box 643), 02651. Professional. Studio/gallery specializes in Ed Deegan's one-of-a-kind rings in 14- and 18-karat gold with precious stones. Also features other gold jewelry. Other selections include Kay Deegan's Oshibana (flower collage). Prices range from $2 to $2,000. "We sell only what we make and the shop houses our studios. The quality of our work and the atmosphere of the gallery bring our customers back year after year."

Open May and June, Monday through Saturday 10 to 5; July and August, same hours plus Sunday; September and October, Monday through Saturday 10 to 5; November through April, by appointment only. **Directions:** From Route 6 in Eastham, take Massasoit Road north just past Sheraton Ocean Park Motel. Serendipity is about 2 miles ahead (toward Provincetown) on the left, in a 250-year-old ¾ Cape Cod home. (617) 255-3274.

NORWELL

Norwell Art Complex, 25 Washington Street, 02061. Professional. Selections include porcelain, stoneware, gold and silver jewelry, weaving, blown glass, woodcarvings, and unusual wall decorations. Pieces cost $2 to $350 and up. The complex is in an eighteenth-century house, and comprises many individual galleries, with additional space set aside to simulate rooms in a home. Visitors may watch jewelry being made.

Open all year, Monday through Saturday 10 to 6, Sunday 1 to 5; plus Thanksgiving to Christmas, daily 10 to 8. **Directions:** The complex is just around the corner from the junction of routes 228 and 53, on the left side of Route 53. (617) 878-9156.

The Terry Pottery, 32 Walnut Road, 02061. Professional. Shop features a large assortment of both functional and uniquely decorative hand-built and wheel-thrown stoneware. Prices range from $12 to $200.

Open by appointment only. (617) 659-7007.

To get to Norwell, take Route 3 south (from Boston) exit 30 onto Route 228; follow Route 228 to Route 53.

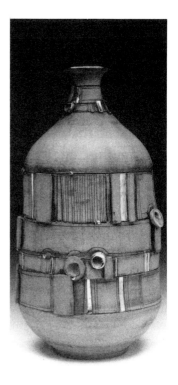

Pottery bottle, The Terry Pottery, Norwell

OAK BLUFFS

Ayn's Shuttle Shop, Wesley House Hotel, Lake Avenue, 02557. Professional. Shop specializes in hand-woven place mats, bags, rugs, and lace window hangings in various designs and sizes. Prices range from $2 to $100. The shop has been in business for more than twenty-five years.

Open May through mid-October, daily 9 to 9. **Directions:** Take the ferry from Woods Hole, Falmouth, or Hyannis to Martha's Vineyard. Lake Avenue is the main street in the village; look for signs to the hotel. (617) 693-0134.

OAKDALE

Apple Ash Pottery, 62 Laurel Street (Box 178), 01539. Professional. Shop specializes in functional stoneware and porcelain, including flat plates and dishes, with hand-painted landscapes a specialty. Other popular hand-painted designs include fish and flowers. Prices range from $2.50 to $100. Ania Monkiewicz gives each piece individual attention, and the result is usefulness plus originality in painting and drawing.

Open all year, by appointment only. (617) 835-3688.

ORLEANS

Artists and Craftsmen's Guild of the Outer Cape Crafts Shows, Nauset Middle School, Route 28. 5 juried fairs: Saturday and Sunday of Memorial Day

To get to Orleans, take Route 6 to exit 12 or to the Orleans rotary.

*Pitcher, Ania Monkiewicz
Studio, Oakdale*

weekend, the first Wednesday and Thursday in July, the first Wednesday and Thursday in August, Saturday and Sunday of Columbus Day weekend, and the second Saturday in December. All are sponsored by the guild (c/o Benjamin Sawin, 101 Morris Island Road, Chatham, 02633). Hours: 10 to 5. About 50 professional and amateur craftspeople and artists exhibit and demonstrate jewelry, leather, metalwork, painting, paper cutting, pottery, decoupage, fiber crafts, and hand-painted purses. Several hundred thousand visitors annually. Admission free. **Directions:** Follow signs, which are posted throughout town. (617) 945-2661.

Ethel Putterman Gallery, Route 6A (Box 766), 02653. Professional. Gallery features the works of forty craftspeople and artists "known for their artistic excellence and originality." Included are contemporary American folk arts and crafts, and abstract and non-objective American paintings and prints. Prices range from $5 to $3,500. The gallery also offers tours describing the processes used in crafts and art production, and demonstrations of techniques.

Open all year, Monday through Saturday 10 to 5; Sunday from 1 (but closed Wednesday, September through May). **Directions:** Take exit 12 off Route 6, and follow signs to Route 6A. The gallery is next door to Governor Prence Motor Inn. (617) 255-5110.

Orleans Carpenters, Rock Harbor Road (Box 107C), 02653. Professional. Shop specializes in Shaker boxes and other Shaker and colonial reproductions in wood. Selections include boxes in nine sizes, tables, bonnet racks, mirrors, kitchen implements, peg boards, cutting boards, and large items such as hutch tables and cedar chests. Prices range from 25¢ to $600.

Open all year, daily 8 to 5. **Directions:** Take Route 6 to exit 12. Turn right, and go 1½ miles to the second traffic light. Then turn left onto Main Street, and go about ¾ mile; the shop is on the right, and is marked by an oval blue sign. (617) 255-2646.

Stephen F. Gallant, Goldsmith and Jeweler, routes 6A and 28, Boardwalk on the Cove (Box 953), 02653. Professional. Gallant features his own line of jewelry created in the shop, including 14-karat gold and sterling silver pieces. Diamonds, sapphires, and other precious gems are used in his creations. He also carries scrimshaw, pottery, fiber crafts, and wood items, all produced by local Cape Cod craftsmen. Prices range from $5 to $500. Shop atmosphere emphasizes direct customer contact with jeweler-designer Gallant, who can create one-of-a-kind designs as well as his own concepts in metal. Contemporary as well as classic designs and techniques are utilized.

Open July 4 through September 4, Monday through Friday 10 to 9, Saturday to 6; off season, Tuesday through Saturday 10 to 5. **Directions:** The shop is located at the intersection of routes 6A and 28, just ½ mile from the Orleans rotary. (617) 255-2944.

Tree's Place, routes 6A and 28, 02653. Professional. Shop features pottery by Peter Hirsch, Bill and Lesley Reich, David Davis, Rosemary Taylor, and John and Betsy Powel; glass by Fred Meyer; ceramic tiles by Joan Wye and others; porcelain by Brian Segal; art deco jewelry by Rose Fox; designer jewelry by Anne Dick, Silvia Davatz, and others; and wooden tables by Zenya Wild. Prices range from $5 to $100. Emphasizes an "extraordinary selection of ceramic tiles from world resources."

Open Memorial Day through Columbus Day, daily 9:30 to 5:30; rest of year, Monday through Saturday 10 to 5. **Directions:** Exit from Route 6 at Eastham/Orleans rotary. Return ½ mile toward Orleans on Route 6A to intersection with Route 28. The shop is midway between Hyannis and Provincetown, about 25 minutes from each. (617) 255-1330.

PELHAM

Cohen Pottery, 113 Amherst Road, 01002. Professional. Michael and Harriet Cohen specialize in functional stoneware, especially dinnerware, decorated casseroles and tableware, bread baskets, vases, and planters. Prices range from $6 to $100. The Cohens use their special printing techniques in decorating.

Open all year, by appointment only. (413) 256-8691.

PEMBROKE

Milkweed Pod, 95 Church Street, 02359. Professional and amateur. Selections include functional and decorative pottery, jewelry in silver and gold, miniatures, hand-screened software mobiles, knit wear, and stained glass. Prices range from $5 to $75. Items featured at Milkweed Pod are original and "different."

Open all year, Tuesday through Saturday 10 to 6. **Directions:** From Boston, take Route 3 south, and exit onto Route 139. Head west (toward Hanover); the shop is 1 mile ahead, on the left. (617) 293-5297.

PETERSHAM

Petersham Craft Center, North Main Street, 01366. Professional and amateur. Items include paintings in all

Candle holder, Orleans Carpenters, Orleans

media, pottery, jewelry, pewter, woven goods, stained glass, miniature furniture and accessories, herbs, paper goods, stuffed toys, wooden products, quilts, and baskets. Prices range from $1 to $200. Crafts are produced both on the premises and elsewhere in the area.

Open April through mid-December, Tuesday through Saturday 1:30 to 5. **Directions:** Take Route 2 Petersham exit to Route 32, and follow Route 32 to town. (617) 724-3415.

PLYMOUTH

Cat's Paw Pottery, 44 Samoset Street, 02360. Professional. Shop specializes in stoneware hand crafted on the premises: one-of-a-kind sculptural and functional pieces, and popular and functional ware for home use. Items include wind chimes, lamps in traditional and contemporary styles, cookie jars, mugs, canisters, match holders, baking ware, and wall pockets. The wall pockets, vases that hang on walls, are created with an oxide design on a raw clay surface with impressions of dried flowers imbedded in the fired clay. Personalized orders for mugs are accepted. Prices range from $2 to $90. The pieces are the work of Catherine Nissle, an artist/potter who brings a broad background in sculpture and painting to the pottery-making process. She places special emphasis on the use of an unglazed design that she prefers for its broad appeal. She points out the natural look afforded by the unglazed pieces and states that it goes with a wide variety of styles. Demonstrations are given. "With due respect for tradition, I cultivate a creative, innovative product."

Open all year, Monday through Saturday 10 to 5:30; often open additional days and hours. **Directions:** The pottery is located at the eastern end of Route 44, near the center of town, about halfway between routes 3 and 3A, on the right. (617) 746-3835.

To get to Provincetown, take Route 6 to the tip of Cape Cod.

PROVINCETOWN

Cornucopia Crafts/Richard Kaish, 348A Commercial Street (Box 1203), 02657. Professional. Shop sells welded bronze as well as brass castings, sterling silver, and 14-karat gold. Available are fantasy pendants and necklaces; sculpture; and bronze necklaces, bracelets, and rings. Also has a complete line of gifts with nautical themes. Prices range from $2 to $700. The pieces of jewelry sold are often one of a kind. The artist works directly in metal to obtain a sculptured look.

Open by appointment only. (617) 487-2057.

RANDOLPH

The Cat's Pajamas Pottery, 31 Pauline Street, 02368. Professional. Shop specializes in functional stoneware: dinnerware, casseroles, gravy pots, honey pots, platters, goblets, and vases. The stoneware is produced in both brown and white, with underglaze pencil designs. Prices begin at $4. All pieces are of "exquisite craftsmanship and attractive design," and the potter makes use of both matte and shiny glazes in unusual colors.

Open by appointment only. (617) 986-5222.

SAGAMORE

Briar Patch Sterling, 103 Canal Road, 02561. Professional. Susan Doucette offers her own jewelry in gold and precious stones. Prices range from $25 to $2,500. Doucette emphasizes that her designs are one-of-a-kind: "I hate doing anything twice — I won't even make earrings if I can help it!"

Open by appointment only. (617) 888-2393.

SALEM

To get to Salem, take any of the Salem exits from Route 128.

A.B.L.E.'s Handcrafts of New England, Salem Market, 01970. Professional and amateur. Shop features afghans, nautical lamps, crocheted toys, dolls, braided rugs, quilts, puzzles, doll houses, doll-house furniture, sweaters, hats, mittens, and wood inlays. Prices range from 65¢ to $200. A.B.L.E. is a VISTA non-profit organization selling the work of low-income New England crafters. It is the only such program in the country that deals with a multi-state region.

Open all year, Monday through Saturday 10 to 6, Sunday noon to 5. **Directions:** Salem Market is opposite the old town hall. (617) 744-9633.

Erika Murray, 21 Flint Street, 01970. Professional. Murray weaves and sells rugs of all sizes from doormats to room-sized pieces. Also carries place mats, pillows, and throws. Prices range from $1 to $720.

Open by appointment only. (617) 745-6728.

SALISBURY

Divided House of Gifts, 255 Elm Street, 01950. Professional and amateur. Shop specializes in handmade doll houses and doll-house furniture. Prices range from $5 to $5,000. The shop's artisans create their own designs for doll houses, and execute those designs on the premises.

Open December 26 through February, Tuesday through Saturday 10 to 6, except open Friday to 9;

March through June, Tuesday through Saturday 10 to 6, except open Friday to 9, Sunday noon to 4; July to Christmas, Monday through Saturday 10 to 6, except open Friday to 9, Sunday noon to 4. **Directions:** Take Interstate 95 exit onto Route 110E toward Salisbury Beach. The shop is about ½ mile ahead on the right. (617) 462-8423.

Footstool, Amidon Wood-carving, Sandwich

SANDWICH

Amidon Woodcarving, (gallery) 139 Main Street, (workshop) 376 Route 130, 02563. Professional. Shop features hand-carved wooden signs and decorative accessories. Also carries original stools and tables, lamps, and wind chimes in wood and metal. Prices begin at $1 and reach into the thousands. A specialty is wooden items — footstools, bar stools, lamps, and book ends — carved to look like feet and hands.

Gallery open June through September, daily 10 to 5; off season, by appointment only. Workshop open all year, Monday through Friday 8:30 to 5. **Directions:** To get to workshop, take Route 6 exit 2 onto Route 130, then follow Route 130 south for about 1½ miles. To get to the gallery, turn left off Route 130 onto Main Street. (617) 888-0565.

SANTUIT

Buckleworks, junction routes 28 and 130 (Falmouth Avenue), 02635. Professional. Shop features two crafts businesses, one selling brass buckles and sterling buckles in about seventy designs, the other selling handmade shearling (sheepskin) jackets, slippers, mitts, hats, and seat covers. Prices range from $10 to $295.

Open all year, Monday through Saturday 9 to 5; additional hours by appointment. **Directions:** The shop is next to the home of Joseph and Anne Barrett. (617) 428-5374.

SOUTH CHATHAM

Heller-Moore Stained Glass, 2092 Main Street (Box 255, West Chatham, 02669). Professional. Shop features stained-glass hanging panels, windows, mirrors, and boxes. Artist Susan Heller-Moore uses cooper foil technique with imported glass. Pieces cost $10 to $500 and up. All designs are Heller-Moore's own — from unusual shell motifs to custom-made architectural pieces.

Open May through mid-October, Tuesday through Sunday 10 to 6; mid-October through April, Tuesday through Sunday 1 to 5. **Directions:** Take Route 6 exit

11, then turn left onto Route 137. Follow it to Route 28, and turn left. The studio is less than ½ mile from the junction of routes 137 and 28.

SOUTH DARTMOUTH

Slocum River Pottery, 452 Potomska Road, 02748. Professional. Leslie Powell specializes in functional stoneware and porcelain for the table and kitchen. Prices range from $5 to $50. "I use a beautiful green glaze in decorating and, as my studio is near the ocean, I use many fish motifs."

Open all year, by chance or appointment; please call ahead. **Directions:** Take Interstate 195 North Dartmouth exit. Go past malls and through a large intersection to a fork in the road (Chase Road). Follow Chase Road to the end, then take a right onto Russells Mills Road and go 1 mile. Turn left onto Rock-O-Dundee Road. Go 1 mile, and bear right onto Potomska Road. Powell's studio is 1½ miles ahead. (617) 994-4216.

SOUTH DENNIS

Fiber Works, 6 Holly Street, 02660. Professional and amateur. Studio specializes in original macramé designs for window and door curtains, wall pieces, lamp shades, plant holders, handbags, belts, and jewelry. Prices range from $5 to $150. Emphasizes originality and choice of materials — "different from what most people use; you name it, I'll knot it!"

Open all year, by appointment only; please phone ahead. (617) 394-2460.

SOUTH HARWICH

Paradise Pottery, 928 Main Street, 02661. Professional. Shop specializes in quality functional stoneware, including mugs, casseroles, vases, serving dishes, and storage jars. Work is hand decorated by sgraffito and in antique-lace patterns. Prices range from $2 to $150. Everything is handmade on the premises. "Our pottery is designed to be functional first but decorative, too. We guarantee everything we make."

Open daily all year. "Call ahead to make sure we are here." **Directions:** Take Route 6 Chatham/Harwich exit to Route 137. Head south on Route 137 to Route 28, then turn west onto Route 28. The shop is 1½ miles ahead. (617) 432-1713.

SOUTHWICK

Eric Jensen, Stringed Instruments, 352 Granville Road, 01077. Professional. Eric Jensen's specialty is

To get to Southwick, take Interstate 91 to the Southwick/Agawam exit onto Route 57 west.

guitars, of which he offers steel stringed, classical, acoustic, and solid-body electric. The solid-body electric guitars are uniquely styled for design and playability. Also featured are basses and dulcimers. Prices range from $95 to $700. "These instruments are not imitations of factory designs, but are professionally built to suit individual customers' tastes. Each piece of work is distinctive, and no two are exactly alike."

Open all year, by appointment. (413) 569-6836.

Grasshopper Greenery/Irene Jensen, 352 Granville Road, 01077. Professional. Shop specializes in unique and distinctive dried-herb-and-silk floral arrangements. Jensen uses home-grown plants, silk flowers, fruits, and other natural products. Prices range from $10 to $44. Jensen's creative arrangements reflect a decorative, whimsical flair. "My ideas are original and enhance what nature has to offer."

Open all year, by appointment only; please call ahead. (413) 569-6836.

SOUTH YARMOUTH

Vinland Patchwork/Amanda Barabe, 94 Blue Rock Road, 02664. Professional. Studio specializes in patchwork kits of all kinds, including pillows in a variety of patterns, quilts, tote bags, pocketbooks, belts, and wall hangings. Will custom make quilts and pillows. Items cost $3 to $60 and up. Barabe stresses precision in piecing fabrics together, and creative use of color.

Open all year, by appointment only. (617) 398-0261.

To get to Springfield, take Interstate 91.

SPRINGFIELD

Annual Antique and Craft Show, Jewish Community Center, 1160 Dickinson Street, 01108. A 1-day juried crafts event, sponsored by the Women's Section of the center and held the second or third Sunday in November. Hours: 10 to 5. About 100 professional and amateur craftspeople exhibit pottery, leather, lapidary, marquetry, batik, jewelry, wood, stained glass, and calligraphy. Demonstrations of pewter engraving and weaving. 3,500 visitors annually. Admission charge. **Directions:** Take Interstate 91 Longmeadow exit, and follow Route 5 to Converse Street. Turn onto Converse Street, and go about 1½ miles to the center, which is on the corner of Dickinson and Converse streets. (413) 739-4715.

Annual Big Fourth Festival, 1618 Main Street, 01103. A 4-day juried crafts fair, sponsored by the Mayor's Office for Cultural and Community Affairs and held from Friday through Monday of the Fourth of July weekend. Hours: 11 to 8. About 50 professional and amateur craftspeople exhibit stained glass, blown glass, fabric design, and batik. Demonstrations of woodwork and blown glass. 100,000 visitors annually. Admission free. **Directions:** Take Interstate 91 exit at Springfield center, and continue to Main Street. The festival grounds have parking facilities. (413) 787-6620.

Metro Arts, 32 Hampden Street, 01103. Professional. Selections include pottery handmade by area craftspeople, quilts, weaving, batik, gold jewelry, paintings, and photography. Prices range from $10 to $200. Fine quality crafts are offered in "a Quincy Market setting."

Open all year, Tuesday through Saturday 10 to 5, except open Thursday to 7. **Directions:** Take Interstate 91 exit for downtown Springfield. The shop is located 4 blocks north of the Marriot Hotel at Bay State West. (413) 736-2021.

Carved-wood painted mouse, The Green Apple, Sturbridge

STURBRIDGE

The Green Apple, on the common, Route 131, 01566. Professional and amateur. Featured are quilted items, carved-wood mice and rabbits, tole ware with an unusual look, country decorative crafts, and a large variety of dolls and children's clothing. The choice of items is "limited to those of excellent quality and craftsmanship." Pieces are attractively displayed amid antiques, which are also for sale.

Open all year, Monday through Friday 1 to 5:30, Saturday and Sunday from 11:30. **Directions:** Take Interstate 90 exit 9 onto Route 20, and follow Route 20 to the traffic light. Then turn left onto Route 131 and continue to the common. (617) 347-3935, or 347-7303.

TEMPLETON

Templeton Arts and Crafts Festival, the common. 2-day juried crafts festival, sponsored by Templeton Arts and Crafts Festival Committee (c/o Gladys Salame, Barre Road, 01468) and held the fourth Saturday and Sunday of August. Hours: 10 to 5. About 100 professional and amateur craftspeople exhibit wood, stained glass, leather, macramé, jewelry, pottery, forged iron, photography, ceramics, rugs, quilts, caned chairs, blown glass, and silk flowers. 20,000 visitors annually. Admission free. **Directions:** From Route 2, take Baldwinville Road exit or East Templeton exit, then follow Route 2A to the center of town. (617) 939-8402.

TOPSFIELD

To get to Topsfield, take Route 95 to Route 1 or Endicott Road.

New England Crafts Expo, Topsfield Fairgrounds, Route 1. A 3-day juried crafts fair, sponsored by American Crafts Expositions, Inc. (Box 368, Canton, CT 06019) and held the third weekend of June. Hours: Friday noon to 7, Saturday and Sunday 10 to 7. Approximately 250 professionals exhibit crafts in all media, with some demonstrations. Food booths. Performing arts stage. 25,000 visitors annually. Admission charge. **Directions:** Take Route 128 to Route 1, and head north. Follow signs to the fairgrounds. (203) 693-6311.

Studio 70, 70 Washington Street, 01983. Professional. Isabella Groblewski sells her own stoneware pots for both house and garden, as well as her silk-screened prints. Prices range from $2 to $350.
Open all year, by appointment only. (617) 887-5576.

Stoneware candle tower by Isabella Groblewski, Studio 70, Topsfield

TRURO

Albert M. Kaufman Workshop, Castle Road (Box 806), 02666. Professional. Kaufman specializes in wood products handmade in woods from all over the world. Selections include carvings, sculpture, and furniture. "It is a shop dedicated to the love of wood."
Open all year, Monday through Saturday 9 to 5. **Directions:** Take Route 6 to "Pamet Road, Truro Center" sign. Take a right, then two more rights, and bear left onto Castle Road. The workshop is about ¼ mile ahead on the left. (617) 349-2963.

WELLESLEY

The Gifted Hand, 32 Church Street, 02181. Professional. Shop features a unique, changing selection of distinctive American crafts, including an array of Amish and Mennonite quilts. Other items offered are leather handbags, briefcases, and journals; woven shawls and blankets; clothing; jade, cloisonné, sterling, and gold jewelry; soft sculpture; and wooden ware. Prices range from $10 to $1,000. Emphasizes "overall high quality" and a diversity of items.
Open all year, Monday through Saturday 10 to 5:30, except open Thursday to 9. **Directions:** Take Interstate 90 to Wellesley center. The shop is behind Filene's Department Store. (617) 235-7171.

WELLESLEY HILLS

Wellesley Arts and Crafts Guild, Inc. Pre-Christmas Sale, 309 Washington Street. 3-day juried crafts fair, sponsored by the guild (25 Whittier Road, 02181) and held during the first full week of November. Hours: Thursday preview sale 8 PM to 10 PM, Friday 10 to 9, Saturday 10 to 3. About 60 professional and amateur craftspeople exhibit stained glass, pottery, jewelry, miniatures, doll houses, needlework, stitchery, pillows, carved birds, lamp shades, and Christmas crafts. Snack bar Friday 11 to 2. About 800 visitors annually. Admission charge Thursday only. **Directions:** From Route 128, turn west onto Route 16 and continue to the junction with Route 9. The fair is at the Wellesley Hills Unitarian Church, at the junction. (617) 235-6162.

WELLFLEET

Salt Marsh Pottery, East Main Street (Box 311), 02667. Professional. The pottery specializes in bright red and yellow earthenware, both glazed and unglazed stoneware, and turned-wood products. Prices range from $3 to $75.

To get to Wellfleet, take Route 6 toward Provincetown, and turn left at the sign for Wellfleet center.

Open June through August, Wednesday through Sunday 9 to 5; September through May, by appointment only. **Directions:** After turning onto Main Street from Route 6, look for the fourth house on the left — it is marked by a sign. (617) 349-3342.

Secrest Gallery and Craftsmen's Barn, 3 West Main Street (Box 752), 02667. Professional. Shop features contemporary crafts produced by sixty-five American craftspeople. Items include pottery, glass, wood, jewelry, textiles, and metal. Prices range from $1 to $1,000. The Secrests stress the "personalized customer/owner atmosphere of the gallery."

Open June through mid-September, Monday through Saturday 10 to 5:30. **Directions:** After turning onto Main Street, continue through the village to the post office; the shop is next door. (617) 349-6688.

WEST BARNSTABLE

Cedar Swamp Stoneware, 1645 Main Street, 02668. Professional. Shop features a complete line of early-American-inspired stoneware. Prices range from $10 to $110. "Our designs are truly unique in that they are inspired from Old New England antique pottery."

To get to West Barnstable, take Route 6 exit 5 or 6.

Open all year, daily 10 to 5. **Directions:** Take Route 6 exit 6 and turn left onto Route 132. Follow Route 132 to Route 6A, and turn left. Take Route 6A about ½ mile to the shop, which is on the left. (617) 362-9906.

HM Studio, 1636 Route 6A, 02668. Professional. Helen Marks Marvill specializes in individually crafted white clay pottery, in such forms as planters, vases, tiles, jars, teapots and cups, salad bowls, and chowder mugs. Prices range from $5 to $35. This is a small, one-woman studio, where work is done with simple tools to produce a variety of objects in a variety of styles.

Open May through December, Wednesday through Saturday 10 to 4. **Directions:** Take Route 6 exit 5, and head north on Route 149 to Route 6A. The studio is on Route 6A, opposite the fire station. (617) 362-4548.

WEST BROOKFIELD

Summercraft, Salem Cross Inn, Route 9. A 2-day juried crafts fair, sponsored by Patchwork Promotions (Hardwick, 01037) and held the last weekend of July. Hours: 10 to 5. About 70 professional and amateur craftspeople exhibit crafts in many media. Demonstrations of traditional crafts such as spinning, blacksmithing, and broom making are given by crafters from Old Sturbridge Village. Meals and entertainment available. 4,000 visitors annually. Admission charge for adults. **Directions:** Take Interstate 90 exit 9 (Sturbridge), follow Route 148 to Route 9, and turn left. The inn is about 20 minutes ahead. Or, from Interstate 90 Palmer exit, turn left toward Ware, then right onto Route 9, and drive about 30 minutes to the inn. (413) 477-8542, or 477-6422.

WEST SPRINGFIELD

To get to West Springfield and the Eastern States Exposition grounds, take Interstate 91 exit 7, then cross Memorial Bridge to Route 147 west (Memorial Avenue).

Craft Adventure, Eastern States Exposition grounds, 1305 Memorial Avenue, 01089. A 2-day juried crafts fair, sponsored by the Creative Crafts Department, Eastern States Exposition, and held the last weekend in August. Hours: 10 to 8. About 300 professional and amateur craftspeople exhibit many kinds of rugs, weaving, macramé, and embroidery. Demonstrations of rug making, quilting, and needlework. Over 1,000 visitors annually. Admission charge. (413) 732-2361.

Craft Show of Eastern States Exposition, 1305 Memorial Avenue, 01089. A 12-day juried crafts fair, sponsored by the Creative Crafts Department, Eastern States Exposition. Opens on a Wednesday and usually lasts through the third full week of September. Hours: 10 to 10. About 110 professional craftspeople exhibit jewelry, leather, clay, wood, fabric, fiber, glass, and metal. Demonstrations of leather working, jewelry, woodcarving, blown glass, and blacksmithing. Admission charge. (413) 732-2361.

WILLIAMSTOWN

To get to Williamstown, take Interstate 91 exit 26, then follow Route 2 west.

Celebration, Clark Art Institute, South Street. 1-day juried crafts fair, sponsored by the Northern Berkshire Council of the Arts (19 Holden Street, Berkshire Plaza, 01267) and held on Saturday of the Fourth of July weekend. Hours: 10 to 5. About 25 professional craftspeople exhibit leather, stained glass, pottery, stuffed animals, dolls, textile arts, wooden ware, and more. Most crafts are demonstrated. Food available. 500 to 800 visitors annually. Admission free. **Directions:** Take Route 2 to Route 7 (South Street). (413) 663-3651.

The Craft Basket, Colonial Shopping Center, Route 2, 01267. Professional and amateur. Selections include sterling silver and other original jewelry; stained glass; and fiber crafts. Also an extensive collection of woodworks in toys, games, and household pieces. Prices range from $2 to $100. Featured are the works of local New England and New York State craftspeople.

Open all year, Monday through Saturday 10 to 5. **Directions:** The shopping center is midway between the centers of Williamstown and North Adams. (413) 458-8247.

The Jewelers Sun, 115 Water Street, 01267. Professional. Jeweler Tom Ralys offers sterling silver and gold jewelry hand crafted by him in his studio. He also does custom work. Prices range from $5 to $50.

Open all year, Tuesday through Saturday 10 to 5; plus summer, fall foliage, and Christmas seasons, Sunday 10 to 5. **Directions:** Water Street is Route 43 in Williamstown. (413) 458-3270.

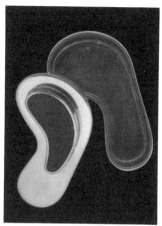

Sterling silver pillbox with ebony inlay by Tom Ralys, The Jewelers Sun, Williamstown

Moon Child Leather, 115 Water Street, 01267. Professional. Margaret Tkal specializes in leather products, including belts, key rings, wallets, and reversible sheepskin hats. Custom work accepted. Prices range from 50¢ to $30, with custom-made items costing more. All work is done on the premises by Tkal, who owns the shop. Her specialty is tooled leather in unique designs, some adapted from Old Norse, and Austrian motifs; in these and other works, she makes widespread use of hand saddle stitching.

Open all year, Tuesday through Saturday 10 to 5; plus summer, fall foliage, and Christmas seasons, Sunday 10 to 5. **Directions:** Water Street is Route 43 in Williamstown. (413) 458-5898.

The Potter's Wheel, Route 43, 01267. Professional. Selections include pottery, woven goods, patchwork quilts, leather bags, and wrought iron. Prices range from $10 to $500. The Potter's Wheel stresses "the high quality of craftsmanship, and our gallery-type display."

Open September through June, daily 10 to 5; July and August, daily 9:30 to 8:30. **Directions:** From Route 2 in the center of town, turn south onto Route 43 (Water Street). The shop is 1 block ahead. (413) 458-9523.

3 Wheelers' Pottery and Gallery, Route 7, 01267. Professional. Gallery specializes in porcelain and stoneware, slab-built and hand-thrown wares — one of a kind pieces made in small-batch production. Specialties are architectural vases, serving platters for fish, small bud vases, and functional wares ranging from mugs to casseroles. Prices range from $3 to $50. This is a working studio shared by three professional female potters, Ann E. Clarke, Joy Friedman, and Terry

Gaberson. Customers can view pottery-making.

Open June through September, Monday through Saturday 10 to 5, Sunday from noon; October through May, daily 9 to 4, but please call ahead. **Directions:** The gallery is on Route 7, about 1½ miles north of the junction of routes 7 and 2, and just south of the Vermont border. (413) 458-4303.

WILMINGTON

William P. Frost, Jr., Woodworker, 260 Lowell Street, 01887. Professional. Frost creates wood products in solid, rare woods. Lamps and bowls are specialties. Prices range from $20 to $200. Frost's one-of-a-kind pieces are unusual in their sizes and shapes.

Open by appointment only. (617) 658-3673.

WOBURN

Abbott Arts, 8 Cedar Street, 01801. Professional and amateur. Selections include fused glass, wooden ware, pottery, weaving, silk screening, ornaments, and knitting and other needle crafts. Items cost $2 to $30 and up. The shop is in an old family homestead in a country setting, where visitors are offered leisurely shopping and even coffee in an old-fashioned kitchen.

Open October through May, Tuesday through Friday 1:30 to 4:30, Saturday and evenings by appointment; June through September, by appointment. **Directions:** Take Route 128 exit 38 onto Washington Street, then turn right onto Cedar Street. (617) 933-0096.

To get to Woods Hole, take Route 28A to Falmouth, then follow signs.

WOODS HOLE

Sixty-Eight Water Street, 68 Water Street (Box 416), 02543. Professional. Shop features stoneware, and wool and mohair weavings. Prices range from $10 to $100.

Open June through October, Monday through Saturday 10 to 4. **Directions:** Follow Route 28 to Water Street, the main street in town. (617) 548-9270.

Under the Sun, 22 Water Street, 02543. Professional and amateur. Selections include functional stoneware by four Cape Cod potters, antique crystal mobiles, pen-and-ink drawings, and wood puzzles for children. Also pewter, crystal, brass, and hand-wrought silver jewelry. Prices range from $3 to $175. Items featured are the work of Cape Cod craftspeople.

Open June through August, daily 9 to 9; September through May, Monday through Saturday 9 to 5:30. **Directions:** The shop is on the main street, Water Street, next to the post office. (617) 540-3603.

WORCESTER

Hammerworks, 75 Webster Street, 01603. Professional. Shop specializes in hand-forged tin — door hardware; cooking utensils; fireplace accessories such as andirons, cranes, and pokers; reflector ovens; crookspout coffeepots; and tin and iron sconces. Also, post lanterns and chandeliers and both traditional and contemporary architectural ironwork such as windows, gate works, and railings. Also produced are spun metal and pewter pieces, and reproduction Windsor chairs in two late-eighteenth-century styles. Custom orders welcome. Prices range from $1.50 to $200. The "only traditional shop in the city, and the only traditional tinsmith within a fifty-mile radius."

Open all year, Monday through Friday 8 to 4, Saturday 8 to noon, and by appointment. **Directions:** Westbound on Interstate 290, take the Hope Avenue exit, and follow Hope Street ¼ mile. Bear right onto Webster Street; the shop is in the former Goddard Gear Works factory building, about ½ mile ahead on the right and marked by a large sign. (617) 755-3434.

Kathleen Schaal Studio, 28 Circuit Avenue East, 01603. Professional. Schaal specializes in wool on cotton-warp flat-woven rugs for both walls and floors. Also sold are colonial coverlets in summer and winter or overshot weaves, plus small pictorial hangings. Prices for rugs range from $300 to $1,000, hangings from $40. Coverlets made by special order.

Open all year, by appointment only. (617) 756-1032.

Leon I. Nigrosh Studio, 11 Chatanika Avenue, 01602. Professional. Nigrosh specializes in wheel-thrown porcelain vessels, luster glazed with precious and semiprecious metallic glazes. Pieces cost $30 to $300 and up. Nigrosh stresses that "few, if any, other clay workers in New England (or nationwide) are working with luster glazes on porcelain ware." The use of classic forms, meticulous care in forming, and finishing are emphasized — finished pieces are "elegant and collectable."

Open all year, by appointment only. (617) 757-0401.

Redwing, an Artisan's Cooperative, 51 Union Street, 01608. Professional. Selections include woven goods, lithographs, calligraphy, soft sculpture, sewn goods, photography, jewelry, and photo-imagery on cloth. Prices range from $5 to $150. The cooperative is a group of eleven local artists producing works for the shop.

Open all year, Monday through Saturday 10 to 6, plus open Wednesday to 9; additional evenings during holiday season. **Directions:** Take Interstate 290 exit 18 (Route 9/Lincoln Square), and go around the rotary to Union Street. The shop is in Union Place, next to Maxwell's Restaurant. (617) 752-1135.

To get to Worcester, take Route 495 or Interstate 90 to Route 290.

Tin lantern, Hammerworks, Worcester

Twenty-four-ounce mug, Pewter Crafters of Cape Cod, Inc., Yarmouth Port

Worcester Craft Center Annual Craft Fair, 25 Sagamore Road, 01605. A 3-day juried crafts fair, sponsored by the Craft Council of the center and held the third weekend of May. Hours: Friday 7 PM to 9 PM, Saturday and Sunday 10 to 6. About 120 professional craftspeople exhibit fiber crafts, ceramics, metal, wood, glass, fabrics, enamel, clothing, and leather. Most crafts are demonstrated. Food available. 6,000 visitors annually. Admission charge. **Directions:** Take Interstate 290 exit 17, then turn left from the ramp into Lincoln Square rotary. Take the second right from the rotary (Salisbury Street); stay to the right and go through the traffic light. Watch for Tweed's Pub on the left; the next left is Sagamore Road. (617) 753-8183.

Worcester Craft Center Craftshop, 25 Sagamore Road, 01605. Professional and amateur. Selections include sterling silver jewelry, wooden ware, enamels, needlepoint, and porcelain. Prices range from $15 to $200. The jewelry exhibited is the work of more than sixty craftspeople. There is a wide variety of crafts to choose from, and many one-of-a-kind pieces.

Open all year, Monday through Saturday 9:30 to 5:30, except closed holidays. **Directions:** Take Interstate 290 exit 17, then turn left from the ramp into Lincoln Square rotary. Take the second right from the rotary (Salisbury Street); stay to the right and go through the traffic light. Watch for Tweed's Pub on the left; the next left is Sagamore Road. (617) 753-8183.

YARMOUTH PORT

Pewter Crafters of Cape Cod, Inc., 927 Main Street, 02675. Professional. Studio features both traditional and contemporary pewter hollowware and jewelry. Prices range from $5 to $200. Each piece reflects "style, quality, craftsmanship, and the pewterer's character!"

Open all year, Monday through Saturday 9 to 5; summer months, to 6. **Directions:** The studio is located on Route 6A, near the Dennis town line. (617) 362-3407.

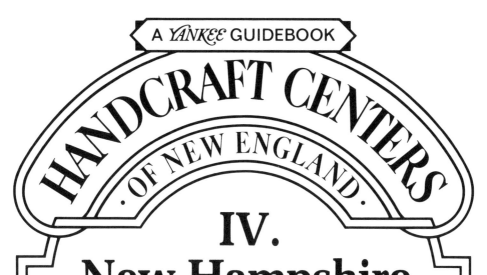

IV.
New Hampshire

The craftspeople of New Hampshire are as geographically scattered as those of any other New England state. But they have something the others don't: a highly respected, long-established crafts organization that includes artisans who work in all media, runs an annual crafts fair in Newbury, and maintains ten shops across the state selling juried merchandise only. It's called the League of New Hampshire Craftsmen, and while it benefits individual craftspeople through its educational programs and sales outlets, it benefits the shopper, too.

There are, of course, craftspeople who live in the Granite State and produce fine crafts but do not happen to belong to the league; a number of them are included here. But when a craftsperson tells you his work has been accepted by a league jury, that's roughly equivalent to his showing you Good Housekeeping's seal of approval; it's your assurance that the work has been judged according to standards maintained throughout the state.

Enamel on copper by Nancy Winzeler, Shop at the Institute, Manchester (see page 121)

BARTLETT

The Beggar's Pouch Leather, Attitash Mountain Craft Village (Box 1056, North Conway, 03860). Professional. Shop specializes in hand-carved and hand-tooled designs on leather, wet-formed sculpture, and originally designed and constructed handbags. Prices range from $1 to $300. Novelty leathers are used, including deerskin, goatskin, sheepskin, and lambskin.

Open Memorial Day through Columbus Day, daily 10 to 5. **Directions:** From Interstate 93, take exit 36 to Route 3 north to Route 302 southeast. The craft village is within Attitash Ski Area. (603) 356-2807.

BROOKFIELD

Stoneham Pewter, Stoneham Corners (RFD 1), 03872. Professional. Shop specializes in pewter produced on the premises by master pewterer Ted White and apprentice Cheryl White. Prices range from $7 to $200.

Open by appointment only; please call or write. (603) 522-3425.

CANAAN

Annual Regional Craftsmen's Fair, on the common. 3-day fair, held the last Friday, Saturday, and Sunday of July and coordinated by Eloise Fahrner (Canaan Street Road, 03741). Hours: from 9 AM each day. 70 to 80 professional and amateur craftspeople display clay, glass, fiber, wood, leather, metal, and macramé. On Saturday, demonstrations of spinning, woodcarving, pottery, and macramé. Food available. Admission free. **Directions:** The common is in the center of town, at the junction of routes 4 and 118. (603) 523-7763.

The Fahr-Cor-Ner, Canaan Street Road, 03741. Professional. Eloise Fahrner specializes in macramé goods such as watch bands, belts, plant hangers, and small wall hangings. Prices range from $3 to $50.

Open all year, by appointment only. (603) 523-7763.

CENTER SANDWICH

Ayottes' Designery, 03227. Professional. Robert and Roberta Ayotte offer their own original designs in a full line of woven apparel — coats, capes, dresses, hostess gowns and skirts, jumpers, ponchos, and jackets. They also feature wall hangings, rugs, lap robes, pillows, and place mats. Prices range from $1 to $500. "Our line of weaving is sold exclusively through this shop."

Open all year, Thursday through Saturday 10 to 5. (603) 284-6915.

Sandwich Home Industries, 03227. Professional and

Tall clock by Lawrence Bickford, Contemporary Furniture, Concord

To get to Center Sandwich, take Interstate 93 exit 23, and follow Route 25 northeast to Moultonborough, then take Route 109 northwest, through Sandwich to Center Sandwich.

amateur. Shop features pottery, lamp shades, iron articles, toys, silver jewelry, woven items, carvings, herb items, crocheted sweaters, prints, ties, cards, and leather. Prices range from $3 to $700. This was the first of the League of New Hampshire Craftsmen shops.

Open end of June through mid-October, daily 9:30 to 5. **Directions:** The shop is at the junction of routes 113 and 109. (603) 284-6831.

To get to Concord, take Interstate 93 exit 13, 14, or 15.

CONCORD

Concord Arts and Crafts, 36 North Main Street, 03301. Professional and amateur. Sells a large variety of items, from blown glass and stained glass to silver and gold jewelry. Also carries pottery, weaving, and knitted goods. Prices range from 50¢ to $700. This is a League of New Hampshire Craftsmen shop; all exhibitors have been juried to insure quality control.

Open all year, Monday through Saturday 10 to 5; summer, Saturday 9 to 1. **Directions:** The shop is on Main Street, opposite Warren Street, on the right when you're driving north. (603) 228-8171.

The Juniper Tree Gallery, Loudon Road, 03301. Amateur. Gallery sells a wide selection of unique items hand crafted by New Hampshire residents; selections include doll furniture, dried-flower arrangements, pottery, stained glass, stenciling, and water colors. Items cost 50¢ to $100 and up. The gallery is a cooperative association of eight New Hampshire artisans.

Open June through August, Wednesday through Saturday 10 to 4:30; September through May, Tuesday through Saturday same hours and also open by appointment. **Directions:** From Interstate 93 exit 14, take Route 4 (Loudon Road) east. The shop is in the OK Garage Craft Shop. (603) 224-7232.

Lawrence Bickford, Contemporary Furniture, RFD 4, North Pembroke Road, 03301. Professional. Bickford specializes in furniture with clean and simple lines, influenced by Scandinavian and Shaker motifs. Each piece is designed to be both handsome and functional, and is then carefully crafted in a hardwood. Selections include love seats, easy chairs, silver chests, and bedroom furniture. Prices range from $25 to $2,500. "Attention to detail, excellent craftsmanship, beautiful wood, and simple and striking designs" are emphasized by Bickford, who is "sensitive to the warmth and beauty of the wood."

Open all year, Monday through Friday 8 to 5:30, Saturday and Sunday occasionally same hours, or by appointment. **Directions:** From Interstate 93 exit 14, drive east 1½ miles. Turn right onto Canterbury Road, then left at the blinking light, onto Pembroke Road. Follow 3.7 miles to house and shop, on the left. (603) 224-9443.

The Mountain Barn, 5 Franklin Street, 03301. Professional. Shop features hand-crafted lamp bases and lighting fixtures made by New England potters and metalworkers. The shop also produces hand-sculptured lamp shades designed to match the individual lamp bases. Prices range from $15 to $50.

Open all year, Monday through Friday 10 to 5, Saturday to noon, plus Monday and Wednesday evenings 7 to 9; closed Sunday and evenings in summer. **Directions:** Take Interstate 93 exit 15 west to North Main Street; turn left onto North Main Street, and then right onto Franklin Street just after Friendly Restaurant. The shop is the first building on the left. (603) 224-5570.

Lamp base and cut-out shade, The Mountain Barn, Concord

CONWAY

Gary Wright, Tasker Hill Road (Box 1661), 03818. Professional. Wright specializes in veneer inlay and marquetry work. Subjects include the J.R.R. Tolkien books and New England landscapes. Wright took first place in the 1981 Marquetry Society of America national competition. Prices range from $150 to $1,500.

Open all year, by chance or appointment. **Directions:** Take Interstate 93 exit 23, then head east on Route 104 to Route 25. Follow Route 25 northeast to Route 16, then take Route 16 into town. At the traffic light, turn right and follow for ½ mile, then bear right and go 1 mile. Turn right onto a dirt dead-end road. Shop is the first barn and house on the right. (603) 447-2375.

DEERING

George Ponzini, Stained Glass, East Deering Road (RR 1, Box 117, Hillsborough, 03244). Professional. Ponzini specializes in Tiffany-type lamps in original designs. Custom orders accepted. Prices range from $20 to $1,000.

Open by appointment only. (603) 529-2761.

DOVER

Red Horse Hill Pottery, 200 Sixth Street, 03820. Professional. George and Cheryl Niles specialize in hand-thrown stoneware and porcelain pottery, including coffee, beer, and chowder mugs; soufflé dishes; colanders; lamp bases; and vases of many sizes. Pottery also done on commission. Prices range from $4 to $100. All pottery is made on the premises in original designs.

Open all year, by chance or appointment. **Directions:** From Interstate 95 exit 6 (Portsmouth), head north on Route 4 to Route 16, then follow Route 16 (Central Avenue) into Dover, and turn onto Sixth Street. Go about 1 mile to the shop, which is in the first house on the left after the overpass. (603) 749-0452.

To get to Durham, take Interstate 93 exit 14, then head east on Route 4. Or, take Interstate 95 north to Route 4, then follow Route 4 northwest.

DURHAM

Elizabeth Nordgren/Design Studio, 6 Ryan Way, 03824. Professional. Studio selections include wall hangings in painted-warp technique, multiharness rugs, tapestries, pillows, and clothing. Prices begin at $25. Features contemporary designs in interesting colors.

Open all year, by appointment only. (603) 868-2873.

University of New Hampshire Annual Christmas Craft Fair, Memorial Union Building. 2-day crafts fair, sponsored by University of New Hampshire Student Activities Office (Room 126, Memorial Union Building, University of New Hampshire, 03824) and held the second Thursday and Friday of December. Hours: 10 to 6. About 50 professional and amateur craftspeople exhibit pottery, jewelry, sculpture, weaving, wood, glass, quilling, tole ware, calligraphy, and macramé. 6,000 visitors annually. Admission free. **Directions:** The fair is held in the Granite State Room of the Memorial Union, which is on the university campus. (603) 862-1001.

EPSOM

The Fire-Fly, Black Hall Road (RFD 1), 03234. Professional. Shop specializes in functional and decorative utensils constructed of hand-wrought brass and mild steel; offerings include measuring-cup and measuring-spoon sets, kitchen utensils with both straight and twisted handles, salad servers, gravy ladles, and racks. Special designs done on commission. Prices range from $4 to $200. All pieces are crafted in unique and delicate designs by two women blacksmiths.

Open all year, by appointment only. (603) 736-8205.

To get to Exeter, take Interstate 95 exit 2 and go west 4 miles on Route 51.

EXETER

Exeter Craft Center, 61 Water Street, 03833. Professional and amateur. Features a wide selection of crafts, from note paper to stained-glass panels. Prices range from $10 to more than $300, with most under $50. This is a League of New Hampshire Craftsmen shop; the league's jury system, at the local as well as the state level, guarantees a very high standard of work.

Open all year, Monday through Saturday 9:30 to 5, plus open Friday to 7. **Directions:** The shop is in the center of town, on Route 101. (603) 778-8282.

Peter C. Lear — Silversmith, 101 Water Street, 03833. Professional. Lear offers his own line of jewelry and other silver items, from small earrings and band rings to large custom pieces such as pitchers, candlesticks, and tea and coffee services. Quotations given. Repairs done. Prices begin at $6, with many in the $25 to $50 range.

Generally open all year, Tuesday through Saturday 10 to 5, but please call ahead. **Directions:** The shop is in the square in the center of downtown, between Indian Head National Bank and Styles' Rexall Drug Store, opposite the bandstand. (603) 772-2422.

FITZWILLIAM

To get to Fitzwilliam, take Route 12 or 119 from Route 202.

Fisher Hill Studios, Fisher Hill, 03447. Professional. Studios specialize in hand-crafted wooden kitchenware and other housewares, with hand-screened designs by Rosalind Welcher. Items include canister sets, cookie boxes, spaghetti boxes, bread boxes, coasters, bookends, and trays. Prices range from $15 to $60. "Designs are of a sophisticated nature, achieving a warmth and quality unobtainable by mass-production methods. The charm of each item is accompanied by a generous helping of New England practicality."

Open all year, Monday through Friday 9 to 5, but please call for an appointment. **Directions:** Take Route 119 to Rhododendron State Park in Fitzwilliam, then continue straight on a dirt road through the woods for ¾ mile, and look for a silver mailbox on the right. The shop is set back 200 feet. (603) 585-6883.

The Pottery Works, Route 119 (Box 345), 03447. Professional. Shop specializes in flameware cooking utensils for use on electric, gas, or wood-burning stoves — frying pans, quiche dishes, pie plates, teapots, and bowls. Also carries porcelain and stoneware place settings, bowls, mugs, and planters. All pieces are wheel thrown or hand built. Prices range from $4 to $48. The Pottery Works has a working studio downstairs and a showroom upstairs. Visitors are welcome to browse, ask questions, and watch the pottery-making process.

Open all year, daily 8 to 5. **Directions:** The shop is located in the section of town called Fitzwilliam Depot, just 1 mile from the Fitzwilliam Inn. (603) 585-6644.

Wooden cookie box with hand-screened design by Rosalind Welcher, Fisher Hill Studios, Fitzwilliam

FRANCONIA NOTCH

League of New Hampshire Craftsmen Craft Shop, Glaessel Building (Box 428), 03580. Professional and amateur. Selections include hand-crafted jewelry, pottery, woodcarving, weaving, stationery, leather, botanical lamp shades, stained glass, blown glass, and macramé. Prices range from $1 to $400. Features the unusual in crafts by over one hundred craftspeople.

Open May through October, daily 9 to 5:30. **Directions:** Take Interstate 93 north to Lincoln, then continue north on Route 3. At the northern end of Franconia Notch, turn left into the parking lot for the Cannon Mountain Tramway, and follow signs to the shop. (603) 823-9521.

Herb and tea mixtures, The Herb Patch, Georges Mills

GEORGES MILLS

The Herb Patch, Prospect Hill Road, 03751. Professional and amateur. Shop specializes in herbs and herb products: original herb mixtures, teas, culinary herbs and blends, potpourris, and bath herbs. Also carries raffia dolls, pottery, dried flowers, handmade incense, room refreshers, fragrance oils, baskets, stained glass, and handmade soft goods. Many items are under $10. "Most everything is original in design and has been hand crafted by local craftspeople."

Open all year (except closed third week in September), Tuesday through Saturday 9 to 5; plus open Memorial Day through Labor Day, Monday 9 to 5. **Directions:** Take Interstate 89 exit 12A, and follow signs to the center of town (about 1 mile). The shop is two doors away from the post office, next to Lee Collins Antiques. (603) 763-4493.

GILFORD

New Hampshire Crafts Festival, Gunstock Recreation Area. 2-day crafts festival, sponsored by the recreation area (Route 11A, 03246) and held the second Saturday and Sunday of July. Hours: 10 to 5. About 150 professional and amateur craftspeople exhibit crystal cutting, photography, painting, blacksmithing, jewelry, leather, weaving, lacquering, and ornamenting of fancy breads. Demonstrations of crystal cutting, woodcarving, basketry, and blacksmithing. 20,000 visitors annually. Admission free. **Directions:** From Interstate 93, take exit 20 to Route 3 east to Laconia. Then take the second exit from Route 3, onto Route 11A, and follow that for 12 miles to Gunstock. The festival is held in the base lodge of the ski area. (603) 293-4341.

GOFFSTOWN

Nancy Lyon Handweaving Studio, 35 North Mast Road, 03045. Professional. Studio/gallery specializes in hand-woven hats, scarves, coats, blankets, pillows, and wall hangings crafted in the studio by the owner. Most items are made of natural fibers; all are either original, limited edition, or one of a kind. Prices range from $20 to $500. Lyon focuses on color and design in weaving luxury fibers such as mohair, silk, and hand-spun wool; also offers visitors the opportunity to see the equipment and materials being used, and to talk with the designer.

Open all year, weekdays by chance or appointment; weekends by appointment only. **Directions:** From Everett Turnpike exit 10, take Route 101 to Route 114, then follow Route 114 to Goffstown. The shop is just north of town, on the left. (603) 497-2084.

GORHAM

Mountain Tapestry, 51 Main Street, 03581. Professional and amateur. Selections include prints as well as locally made crafts of clay, wood, glass, and fiber. Also carries yarns. Prices range from $5 to $100.

Open April through December 24, Monday through Saturday 10 to 5 (except closed Wednesday); January through March, by appointment. **Directions:** Take Route 2 or Route 16 to Main Street. (603) 466-5179.

GOSHEN

Nelson Crafts, Brook Road (RR 2, Box 540, Newport, 03773). Professional. Shop features the works of the Nelson family. Sold here are plates and platters; new designs in hand-woven and hand-knit wool coats and sweaters; hand-sewn garments made from antique lace, silk, linen, cotton, and wool; hand-woven tapestries and pillows; stoneware pottery and sculpture; mosaics; yarns; and hanging planters. Prices range from 25¢ to $500. Visitors welcome to watch work in progress.

Open Memorial Day to Labor Day, daily 10 to 5; Labor Day to Christmas, Saturday and Sunday 10 to 5; other times, by appointment. **Directions:** From Interstate 89 north exit 9, take Route 103 west to the rotary at the entrance to Mount Sunapee State Park. Continue 1 mile farther on the same road; then, at Schweitzer's Restaurant, turn left (south) onto Brook Road. The shop is 3 miles ahead, just beyond Rand Pond. (603) 863-4394.

Stoneware sculpture, Nelson Crafts, Goshen

HAMPSTEAD

Heidi's Glas-Haus, Main Street, 03841. Professional. Shop features stained-glass pieces ranging from small sun catchers to window panels and church windows. Emphasizes the quality of craftsmanship and uniqueness of design in all pieces. All products are guaranteed.

Open all year, Monday through Friday 9 to 5, Saturday to 1. **Directions:** From Interstate 93 exit 3, take Route 111 northeast to Route 121, then go north on Route 121 for 3 miles. (603) 329-5443.

HANCOCK

D.S. Huntington Company, Depot Street, 03449. Professional. Shop specializes in wooden products, ranging from small stools to cabinets and one-of-a-kind pieces of furniture. Items cost $40 to $50 and up. D.S. Huntington offers "absolutely the finest quality workmanship and only the best materials."

Open all year, daily 8 AM to 9 PM. **Directions:** Take Route 202 north to Route 123, then follow Route 123 north through town. Just beyond the town center, turn onto Depot Street. The shop is in a brown house (the first house on the dirt portion of the road), next to a small red barn. (603) 525-6687.

HANOVER

To get to Hanover, take Interstate 91 exit 13 and turn east, across the Connecticut River, to town. To get to Lebanon Street, turn right onto Main Street at the traffic light, then take the first left, at the next traffic light.

The Artifactory, 25 Lebanon Street, 03755. Professional and amateur. Selections include gold and silver jewelry, baskets, wrought-iron ware, functional pottery, blown glass, purses, travel bags, wallets, clogs, lamps, bells, and windchimes. Prices range from $1 to $400. Features "a delightful, ever-changing, ever-evolving presentation of crafts representing the work of seventy-five artists from throughout the nation."

Open all year, Monday through Saturday 9:30 to 5. (603) 643-2277.

League of New Hampshire Craftsmen, 13 Lebanon Street, 03755. Professional and amateur. Shop features weaving, pottery, silver and gold sculpture and jewelry, leaded glass, and woodwork.

Open all year, Monday through Saturday 9:30 to 5. **Directions:** The shop is located directly behind Hopkins Center. (603) 643-5050.

Upper Valley Development and Training Center Benefit Crafts Fair, Hopkins Center plaza. 1-day juried fair sponsored by the training center (West Lebanon, 03784) and held the last Wednesday of August. Hours: 9 to 6. About 80 professional and amateur craftspeople exhibit pottery, blacksmithing, batik, weaving, jewelry, woodcarving, macramé, metal art, embroidery, wooden-toy making, and portraiture. Demonstrations of almost all crafts. Home-baked food available. Thousands of visitors annually. Admission free. **Directions:** From Interstate 91, take the Norwich/Hanover exit and head east into Hanover. Continue straight at the Main Street intersection; Hopkins Center is on the right. (603) 448-2077 or (603) 643-2258.

HENNIKER

The Fiber Studio, Foster Hill Road, 03242. Professional and amateur. Shop features hand-woven mohair stoles, jackets, blankets, wall hangings, and sweaters. Also carries natural dyes and yarns. Prices range from $2 to $100. Weavings are done by local craftspeople.

Open all year, Tuesday through Saturday 10 to 4, Sunday by chance. **Directions:** From Interstate 89 exit 5, take Route 9 west 8 miles. At the state highway sign for the shop, turn right onto Foster Hill Road; the shop is a short way up the hill. (603) 428-7830.

HILLSBOROUGH CENTER

Gibson Pewter, East Washington Road (Box 430, Route 2), 03244. Professional. Sells pewter fashioned in an open shop where visitors are welcome to watch the work in progress. Prices range from $10 to $80. Emphasis is placed on the quality of the metal used and the craftsmanship involved.

Open July and August, daily 9 to 4:30. **Directions:** From Interstate 89 exit 5, take Route 9 west to Hillsborough. In the center of Hillsborough, turn onto East Washington Road; follow this road 3 miles to Hillsborough Center, and watch for the shop sign. (603) 464-3410.

HUDSON

S.B. Viens, 12 Cottonwood Drive, 03051. Professional. Viens specializes in trapunto paintings: each work is painted on muslin, then stuffed and stitched, giving a three-dimensional effect. A variety of subjects is available, ranging from New England countryside scenes to whimsical animal images. Prices range from $10 to $100. Viens says her trapunto is a "unique, seldom-seen craft."

Open all year, by appointment only. **Directions:** From Route 3 exit 1, follow signs to Route 3A. Take Route 3A north to the Blue Whale Restaurant, then turn left. Turn left twice more to get to Cottonwood Drive. (603) 883-5711.

KEENE

Anthony Toepfer, Goldsmith, 13 Roxbury Street, 03431. Professional. Toepfer specializes in original designs in handmade gold jewelry, using either his own or the customer's designs. His line includes everything from simple yet elegant wedding bands to extravagant one-of-a-kind pieces. Prices range from $25 to $1,000.

Open all year, Tuesday through Saturday 10 to 5. **Directions:** The shop is 3 doors away from the town square. (603) 357-3027.

Aurora Designs, Inc., 49 Saint James Street, 03431. Professional. Shop specializes in a unique line of fancy woolen tweeds coordinated with other natural-fiber

Trapunto by S.B. Viens, Hudson

To get to Keene, take Interstate 91 exit 3 (Brattleboro) and drive east on Route 9. Or, take Route 101 west or Route 10 or Route 12 north or south.

119

"Cleopatra," enamel-on-copper pull toy by Nancy Winzeler, Shop at the Institute, Manchester

To get to Manchester, take any exit from Route 293 (Everett Turnpike). Or, take Interstate 93 exit 6, 7, 8, 9, or 10.

fabrics such as cotton, linen, silk, and wool. Also offers a fashion collection of women's apparel. Items are both designed and crafted on the premises. Custom orders accepted for women's apparel. Prices range from $3 to $150. Aurora Designs has "an airy, congenial, studio-like atmosphere, where color and texture abound, delighting the senses and inspiring the mind. Our approach to fashion is tasteful and tailored, accented by a dash of fun."

Open all year, Tuesday through Saturday 10 to 5:30. **Directions:** Saint James Street is parallel to Main Street in the downtown area. The shop is diagonally across from the chamber of commerce and the bus station, on the second floor, above the Square Meal Restaurant. (603) 357-3810.

LACONIA

Pepi Herrmann Crystal, Gilford East Drive, 03246. Professional. Pepi Herrmann features his own hand-cut crystal: vases, goblets, plates, bowls, and trays — both limited editions and one-of-a-kind pieces. Custom orders accepted. Prices range from $10 to $3,000.

Open all year, Monday through Saturday 10 to 5. **Directions:** From Interstate 93 exit 20, take Route 11 to the Laconia bypass; the shop is at the end of the bypass, about 1,000 feet from the road. (603) 528-1020.

LOWER GILMANTON

Killer Bear Pottery, routes 129 and 107 (RFD 2, Pittsfield, 03263). Professional. Shop specializes in porcelain and stoneware pottery designed and produced on the premises. Mostly functional works are produced, including lamps, bowls, plates, pitchers, casseroles, and planters. Prices range from $3 to $100.

Open all year, Tuesday through Saturday 10 to 5. **Directions:** From Interstate 93 exit 14 (Concord), take Route 4 east to Route 106. Take Route 106 north to Route 129, then follow Route 129 north to Route 107. (603) 435-6689.

MANCHESTER

The Color Wheel, 71A Myrtle Street, 03104. Professional. Featured are hand-thrown, high-fired porcelain items, such as lamps, platters, bowls, baking dishes, dinnerware, vases, pitchers, and planters. Prices range from $15 to $60. Potters work with twenty-five to thirty different glazes, including unusual colors and combinations. All work is oven and dishwasher safe, and all glazes are lead free.

Open all year, Monday through Thursday 9 to 4;

other times by appointment. **Directions:** From the Interstate 93 Bridge Street exit in Manchester, head west into town to Pine Street. Go 3 blocks on Pine Street, then turn left onto Myrtle Street. The shop is on the left, 1 block beyond Chestnut Street. (603) 668-5466.

Shop at the Institute, Manchester Institute of Arts and Sciences, 148 Concord Street, 03104. Professional. Shop features carved wood, enamels, jewelry, toys, blankets, sculptures, bells, pewter, and prints. Prices range from $3 to $200. Pieces are completely hand crafted, and are of "extremely fine quality." About half of the crafts featured are produced in New Hampshire, the rest in other New England states.

Open August 15 through June, Monday through Saturday 10 to 5; plus Thanksgiving to Christmas, open Thursday to 9. **Directions:** From Interstate 93 south, take the Amoskeag Bridge exit in Manchester, and follow signs for downtown. At the end of the ramp take a right onto Elm Street, and after about ½ mile turn left onto Bridge Street. Follow Bridge Street to Union Street, then take Union Street to Concord Street. (603) 623-0313.

MASON

Pickity Place, Nutting Hill Road, 03048. Professional and amateur. Shop sells herbs and herbal products, wreaths, herbal draft stoppers, dolls, and children's toys. Prices range from $1 to $100. Visitors can tour formal herb gardens, where over two hundred varieties of herbs — the source of the herbal products made and sold in the shop — are grown.

Open April 15 through December 24, Tuesday through Sunday 10 to 5. **Directions:** From Route 31 south, turn left at the blinking light in Greenville, and follow the signs ½ mile to the shop. (603) 878-1151.

Pole Hill Pottery, 527 Brookline Road, 03048. Professional. Shop features high-fired porcelain made at the studio. Specialties are electric lamps with matching hand-cut lamp shades, and oil and Aladdin lamps with matching mirrors. Prices range from $5 to $100. Pottery and shades are individually designed in "exciting colors — not the same old dull browns. Our seashell handles are totally unique."

Open all year, Monday through Saturday 7 to 4; please call for an appointment. **Directions:** From the blinking light in Brookline, take the road for Parker's Maple Barn; the studio is on the left, 1½ miles past Parker's. (603) 878-2329.

To get to Mason, take Route 101 to Route 31, then head south on Route 31 to Greenville; at the blinking light in Greenville, turn left. Or, take Route 13 to the blinking light in Brookline, then follow the road for Parker's Maple Barn.

MEREDITH

Meredith-Laconia Arts and Crafts, Route 3, 03253. Professional and amateur. Selections include jewelry, pottery, leaded and blown glass, wrought iron, toys, hand knitting, other needlework, and prints. Prices range from 35¢ to $200. This is a League of New Hampshire Craftsmen shop; all pieces are hand crafted by juried New Hampshire craftspeople. Demonstrations are given by league members every Tuesday and Thursday during July and August, from 10 AM to 1 PM.

Open May through December, daily 9:30 to 5:30, except closed Thanksgiving and Christmas days. **Directions:** Take Interstate 93 north to Route 104. Follow Route 104 east to Route 3. The shop is on Route 3, just north of the junction with Route 104. (603) 279-7920.

MERIDEN

Tariki Stoneware, Main Street (Box 172), 03770. Professional. Father-and-son team Jack and Eric O'Leary feature stoneware vases, lamps, mugs, and planters. Tiles for floors and wall murals are a specialty. Commission work accepted. Prices range from $4 to $2,000.

Open all year, Monday through Friday 9 to 5, weekends by appointment. **Directions:** From Interstate 89 exit 18 (Lebanon), take Route 120 south 8 miles to the blinking light in Meriden. Turn left and cross the bridge; the shop is in the first building on the right after the bridge. (603) 469-3243.

To get to Milford, take Route 101 or Route 13.

MILFORD

The Golden Toad Gallery, 65 Elm Street, 03055. Professional and amateur. Selections include batik, sculpture, paintings, prints, metalwork, jewelry, toys, and wooden ware. Prices range from $3 to $300. Features "quality-made and out-of-the-ordinary pieces."

Open all year, Monday through Saturday 10 to 5:30, Sunday from 1. **Directions:** The shop is on Route 101A, about ½ mile west of the center of town. (603) 673-4307.

Impressions/Wildflower Pottery, 21 South Street, 03055. Professional. Bob and Allison Oxford specialize in pottery decorated with impressions of wildflowers. Hand-molded items include dishes, accent pins, napkin rings, ginger-jar lamps, serving platters, bowls, and flowerpots. Prices range from $6 to $110. "We are the only craftsmen in New Hampshire using the impressed-wildflower technique."

Open all year, Tuesday through Saturday 10 to 4. **Directions:** From the center of town, take Route 13 (South Street) south. The shop is in the fourth building on the right. (603) 673-5167.

Joyful Arts, Souhegan Valley Workshop, 47 Elm Street, 03055. Professional and amateur. Selections include hand-rolled beeswax candles in three sizes, wooden candle holders, note cards, hand-knitted toys, and loop tapestries. Prices range from $1.50 to $25.

Open all year, Monday through Friday 9 to 3. **Directions:** From the center of Milford, take Elm Street toward Wilton. (603) 673-7101.

Milford Arts and Crafts Festival, American Stage Festival grounds. 2-day juried crafts festival, sponsored by the Festival Theatre Guild (Box 225, 03055) and held the third Saturday and Sunday of July. Hours: 10 to 5. Approximately 100 professional and amateur craftspeople and artists exhibit pottery, weaving, calligraphy, stenciling, quilting, jewelry, stained glass, photography, and painting. Some crafts are demonstrated. 6,000 to 7,000 visitors annually. Admission free. **Directions:** Take Route 101A or Route 101 to Route 13 north. The American Stage Festival is less than ½ mile from the Milford Oval. (603) 673-3143.

NASHUA

Nashua League of Craftsmen Shop, 95 West Pearl Street, 03060. Professional. Shop features stuffed toys, art prints, pottery, stained glass, hand-crafted jewelry, and wrought iron. Prices range from 50¢ to $325. This is a League of New Hampshire Craftsmen shop; all merchandise is crafted by New Hampshire artisans.

Open all year, Monday through Saturday 9:30 to 5:30. **Directions:** Take Route 3 or Route 101A to Nashua; the shop is in the heart of downtown. (603) 882-4171.

NEWBURY

Annual Craftsmen's Fair, Mount Sunapee State Park, Route 103. A 6-day juried crafts fair, sponsored by the League of New Hampshire Craftsmen (205 North Main Street, Concord, 03301) and held the first Tuesday through Sunday of August. Hours: 10 to 5. About 100 professional craftspeople exhibit pottery, jewelry, metal smithing, weaving, cards, wood, fabric, lamp shades, stained glass, leather, prints, and toys. Also paintings from the New Hampshire Art Association. Crafts demonstrated include pottery, spinning, weaving, and woodworking. 35,000 visitors annually. Admission charge for adults; no charge for children under twelve. **Directions:** From Interstate 89, follow signs to Mount Sunapee State Park. (603) 224-3375.

NEWFIELDS

Ray LaBranche, the Newfields Potter, Route 85 (Box 183), 03856. Professional. Shop specializes in functional stoneware pottery, including mugs, baking dishes, steamers, chandeliers, and nearly one hundred

Stoneware teapot, Tariki Stoneware, Meriden

Botanical casting, Artisan's Workshop, New London

different pots. Prices range from $5 to $80. Visitors are given the opportunity to see pots being made and fired.

Open all year, daily 9 to 5. **Directions:** The shop is about 3 miles north of Exeter. (603) 772-4658.

NEW LONDON

Artisan's Workshop, Main Street, 03257. Professional and amateur. Shop features "a fine selection of stoneware from northern New England potters," and also offers hand-crafted sterling silver and beaded jewelry, small stained-glass items, cards, wooden toys, potpourri, and prints and paintings from area artists, as well as other crafts from local artisans. Prices range from $2 to $150. The shop is housed in an early American inn.

Open all year, daily 9:30 to 5, plus open summer evenings to 9, and selected fall evenings from Labor Day through December to 9. **Directions:** Take Interstate 89 exit 11 (Route 11) and follow posted signs to town. The shop is centrally located on Route 11, in the same building as Peter Christian's Tavern. (603) 526-4227.

NORTH CHATHAM

Cold River Designs, Route 113 (Route 113, North Fryeburg, ME 04058). Professional. Shop features vests and hooded jackets in wool and cotton — all with blanket-stitching. Prices range from $30 to $150. "The 'Chatham jacket' and 'Chatham vest' are unique."

Open by appointment only. (603) 694-3217.

NORTH CONWAY

To get to North Conway, take Route 16 and/or Route 302.

The Beggar's Pouch Leather, Main Street (Box 1056), 03860. Professional. Shop specializes in hand-carved and hand-tooled designs on leather, wet-formed sculpture, and originally designed and constructed handbags. Prices range from $1 to $300. Novelty leathers are used, including deerskin, goatskin, sheepskin, and lambskin.

Open all year, Monday through Saturday 10 to 5:30. **Directions:** The shop is located at the junction of routes 16 and 302, across from the park. (603) 356-2807.

League of New Hampshire Craftsmen, Route 16 (Box 751), 03860. Professional and amateur. Selections include pottery, jewelry, stained and blown glass, appliqué, turned-wood goods, and small wood sculptures. Prices range from 40¢ to $500. "Our handcrafted items are both functional and aesthetic."

Open all year, daily 9 to 5:30. **Directions:** The shop is located just south of the village on Route 16 (near the Conway Scenic Railroad). (603) 356-2441.

NORTHFIELD

Hatfield Stained Glass Studio, Route 132, 03276. Professional. Shop specializes in Don Feldhusen's stained-glass artistry in lamp shades, clocks, mirrors, window hangings, sconces, bowls, dishes, boxes, and planters. Prices range from $10 to $600.

Open all year, Tuesday through Saturday 10 to 5. **Directions:** Take Interstate 93 exit 18, turn left at the first intersection, then left again at the next intersection and left onto Route 132. Go 4 miles to the shop, which is on the left. (603) 286-4908.

NORTHWOOD

To get to Northwood, take Interstate 93 exit 14 to Route 4 east.

Brown Owl Craft Center, Route 4, 03261. Professional and amateur. Center features dolls, holiday decorations, quilts, cradles, rocking horses, and an array of stenciled items — together representing over one hundred craftspeople. Prices range from 60¢ to $225.

Open all year, Wednesday through Monday 9 to 5. **Directions:** The center is about 20 miles from Interstate 93. (603) 942-7636.

Northwood Stoneware Pottery, Route 4, 03261. Professional and amateur. Owner Jeffery Lalish offers his own pottery made on the premises in eighteenth- and nineteenth-century styles. Also features cloth crafts, photography, and paintings of other local craftspeople and artists. Prices range from $5 to $200.

Open all year, Monday through Saturday 10 to 5. **Directions:** The shop is located at the intersection of routes 4, 202, and 9, across the street from the First Baptist Church. (603) 942-8829.

PETERBOROUGH

To get to Peterborough, take Route 3 north to exit 7W, then take Route 101A west to Route 101. Follow Route 101 west to Peterborough. Or, take Interstate 89 exit 5 and follow Route 202 south.

Folkway Craft Shop, 85 Grove Street, 03458. Professional and amateur. Selections include weaving, pottery, wooden and cloth toys, handmade clothing, candles, wrought iron, stained glass, dried-flower wreaths, and jewelry in silver, brass, pewter, ceramics, and macramé. Prices range from 75¢ to $350. This is a "small shop featuring local quality crafts."

Open all year, Tuesday through Saturday 11:30 to 4:30. **Directions:** Take Route 101 west to the traffic light in Peterborough, and turn right onto Grove Street. The shop is in the fifth building on the left. (603) 924-7484.

Pocketful of Rye, 107 Wilton Road, 03458. Professional. Shop features dried floral designs; spice crafts; potpourri sachets; and pomanders. Prices range from $3.50 to $50. Colonial herbal designs are a specialty. Many of the materials used are home grown.

Open April through December 24, daily 10 to 5. **Directions:** The shop is 1 mile east of the center of Peterborough on Route 101, in the same building as the Carousel Horse. (603) 924-7906.

Tewksbury's Art Gallery and Handcraft Shop, Route 101. Shop features pottery, enameled-copper and silver jewelry, and hand-woven scarves and stoles; also carries copper and brass lanterns, clocks, copper water fountains, ceramic lamp bases, and mobiles. Prices range from $5 to $200. Owner-craftspeople Ted and Roberta Tewksbury stress "overall high quality," and emphasize the works of New England craftspeople.

Open January through June, Tuesday through Saturday 10 to 5; July through December, Monday through Saturday 10 to 5, Sunday 1 to 5. **Directions:** The shop is just east of town. (603) 924-3224.

To get to Portsmouth, take Interstate 95 exit 7.

PORTSMOUTH

Annual Street Fair, downtown streets. 1-day crafts fair, sponsored by Theatre-by-the-Sea (125 Bow Street, 03801) and held the first Saturday in August. Hours: 10 to 6. Approximately 150 professional craftspeople exhibit and demonstrate jewelry, woodcarving, pottery, pen-and-ink art, sculpture, and small crafts. Entertainment changes hourly. 8,000 to 10,000 visitors annually. Admission free. **Directions:** From Interstate 95, take any Portsmouth exit and follow strawberry signs to the downtown area. (603) 431-5846.

Christmas at Strawbery Banke, Strawbery Banke, Marcy Street, and other Strawbery Banke houses in the downtown area. 3-day juried crafts festival, sponsored by the Guild of Strawbery Banke and the Restoration Association (Box 523, 03801), and held Friday through Sunday of the second weekend in November. Hours: 10 to 5. About 35 professional craftspeople exhibit and demonstrate silver, pewter, weaving, wood, basketry, hand-mounted tapestries, and silk screened goods. Home-baked goods are available at each stop. Several thousand visitors annually. Admission charge at individual houses. **Directions:** From Interstate 95, take any Portsmouth exit and follow strawberry signs to Strawbery Banke. (603) 436-8032.

The Potter at Strawbery Banke, Strawbery Banke, Marcy Street (Box 300), 03801. Professional. E.H. Wheeler specializes in stoneware pottery for the home: traditional jugs, large cider jugs, bread-mixing bowls, crackle-glaze pitchers, dinner sets, and teapots. Special orders welcome. Prices range from $4 to $120.

Open all year, Tuesday through Sunday 9:30 to 5. **Directions:** From Interstate 95, take any Portsmouth exit and follow the strawberry signs to Strawbery Banke. (603) 436-1506.

Salamandra Glass, 143 Market Street, 03801. Professional. Shop specializes in blown glass — vases, decorative bulls' eyes, tumblers, bowls, and jewelry. Prices range from $20 to $300. Most of the wares in the shop are hand crafted in the adjacent studio; "all items are one-of-a-kind pieces that have been signed and dated."

Open all year, Monday through Saturday 10 to 5 and occasionally on Sunday. **Directions:** From Interstate 95 north exit 7, turn right onto Market Street. (603) 431-4511.

Warg Designs, 33 Bow Street, 03801. Professional. Shop specializes in one-of-a-kind jewelry and functional objects made of both precious and nonprecious metals. Custom orders accepted for jewelry. Prices range from $15 to $300. All items are designed and executed by owner-craftsperson Pauline Warg.

Open all year, Tuesday through Saturday 10 to 6. **Directions:** Take Interstate 95 north exit 7, turn right onto Market Street, and turn left onto Bow Street. (603) 431-5578.

POTTER PLACE

Wild Pottery, Depot Street (Box 82), 03265. Professional. Shop specializes in owner Sam Wild's stoneware pottery made on the premises. Offerings include mugs, flower arrangers, jardinières, hanging planters, teapots, coffee servers, and honey pots. Prices range from $6 to $40. Wild's designs are hand painted in light blue and brown on white backgrounds.

Open all year, by chance or appointment. (603) 735-5658.

RINDGE

Appleton Pottery and Craft Shop, Route 202 (Box 212), 03461. Professional. Shop specializes in wheel-thrown functional and decorative pottery created on the premises. Selections include carefully crafted and glazed lamp bases (also available wired with shades), casseroles, bowls, and unusual flower containers, planters, kitchen accessories, and oven ware. Also carries jewelry, candles, prints, cards, and other items crafted in the region. Prices range from $2 to $150. Pieces are tastefully displayed.

Open April through June, Tuesday through Saturday 10 to noon and 2 to 5; July and August, Monday through Saturday 10 to 5; September through November, Tuesday through Saturday 10 to noon and 2 to 5; month of December, Monday through Saturday 10 to 5. **Directions:** Take Route 202 to Jaffrey or Rindge; the shop is near the Jaffrey/Rindge town line. (603) 532-6015.

Pottery lamp base with shade, Appleton Pottery and Craft Shop, Rindge

To get to Rumney, take Interstate 93 exit 26, then follow Route 25 north.

RUMNEY

"Friends of the Sheep" Fiber Studio and Baker Valley Bead Works, Buffalo Road (Box 290), 03266. Professional. Shop specializes in hand-spun and vegetable-dyed wool yarns; woven, knitted, and crocheted sweaters, caps, shawls, and throws; and unique strung-bead jewelry. Prices range from $4 to $50. All wool is from the studio's own black sheep.

Open by appointment only. (603) 786-9815.

Hellfire Forge, Buffalo Road, 03266. Professional. Studio features hand-forged ironware by owner Brian Cummings, including pieces in mild steel, high-carbon steel, and stainless steel. His line includes lighting devices, cooking utensils, flatware, fireplace equipment, and assorted building hardware. Prices range from $6.50 to $525. Cummings's ironware is very delicate and is made entirely by hand; no power tools whatsoever are used.

Open all year, by chance or appointment. **Directions:** From Interstate 93 exit 26, take Route 25 to the second blinking yellow light. Turn right, then take the second left, onto Buffalo Road. The forge is on the right, 1½ miles from Rumney village. (603) 786-9753.

To get to Sanbornton, take Interstate 93 north exit 20 or 22.

SANBORNTON

Thomas Kuhner, Goldsmith/Silversmith, Route 3B, Sanbornton Square (Box 171), 03269. Professional. Kuhner specializes in hand-crafted jewelry using 14-karat gold, sterling silver, 12-karat-gold-filled metal, and both precious and semiprecious stones. Custom orders accepted. Prices range from $2.50 to $500. "Designs are stylish yet simple, and are made to be affordable."

Open all year, Monday through Saturday by appointment only. **Directions:** Take Interstate 93 north exit 20, then take Route 132 north 3 miles to Sanbornton Square; watch for a sign. (603) 286-3363.

SHARON

Sharon Arts Center, Route 123 (RFD 2, Box 361), 03458. Professional and amateur. Shop features sun-print quilts, Shaker boxes, Robert and Virginia Warfield's carved birds, and silver and gold jewelry. Prices range from $1 to $500. The center is a member of the League of New Hampshire Craftsmen.

Open May through December, Monday through Friday 10 to 5:30, Saturday 10 to 5, Sunday 1 to 5. **Directions:** Take Route 101 to Route 123, then go south on Route 123 for 4 miles. The Sharon Arts Center is on the right. (603) 924-7256.

SOUTH ACWORTH

Gail Ann Duggan, Doll Workshop, the Village Store, 03607. Professional. Studio specializes in original, handmade porcelain dolls. Prices range from $150 to $250. Dolls and accessories are not made from commercial molds; all parts are original. A current popular set, "The Tea Party," features two handmade wooden children at a handmade table. Dolls are exhibited in the store, and the upstairs studio may be visited by chance or appointment.

To get to South Acworth, take Route 10 to Route 123A west.

Open all year, Friday and Saturday by chance or appointment; please call ahead. **Directions:** The Village Store is on Route 123A, just off Route 10 in the center of town. (603) 835-6547.

Marc Goldring/Brenda McCumber — Fine Crafts, Route 123A, 03607. Professional. Shop specializes in dresses, suits, and shirts handmade by Brenda McCumber, using natural silks, wools, and cottons. Also features Marc Goldring's leather work, including vessel forms, bowls, vases, centerpieces, looseleaf binders, pad covers, and belts. Prices range from $10 to $300. The studio deals exclusively in the work of the owners, who emphasize careful and exacting workmanship and innovative approaches.

Open all year, Sunday 10 to 5; other times by chance or appointment. **Directions:** The studio is in the owners' home, on Route 123A in the center of South Acworth, across the field adjacent to the Village Store. (603) 835-6764.

SOUTH WOLFEBORO

Wolfeboro Arts and Crafts, a.k.a. The School House Shop, Route 28 (RFD 1), 03894. Professional and amateur. Selections include stained glass, woodwork, pottery, weaving, wrought iron, tinware, quilted items, pewter, copper enameling, and silver jewelry. Prices range from $1 to $1,000. This is a League of New Hampshire Craftsmen shop, selling only the works of New Hampshire craftspeople.

Open May through December, Monday through Saturday 9:30 to 5:30; also July and August, Sunday 11 to 4. **Directions:** From Wolfeboro, take Route 28 south. The shop is on the right. (603) 569-3489.

STODDARD

Stoddard Glass Studio, Shedd Hill Road, 03464. Professional. Working studio specializes in stained glass, especially ornaments, lamp shades, windows, and models of airplanes. Prices begin at $5.

Open all year, "often but not always." Please call ahead. **Directions:** From Keene, take Route 9 north to

Route 123. Follow Route 123 west to Stoddard, then turn right (north) between the fire station and the post office, and go ⅓ mile to the shop, which is on the left. (603) 446-7015.

SUNAPEE

Sunapee Historical Society Annual Arts and Crafts Festival, school gym, Route 11. A 1-day juried crafts festival, sponsored by the Sunapee Historical Society, Inc. (03782) and held the next to the last weekend in July. Hours: 9 to 5. About 100 professional and amateur craftspeople exhibit ceramics, stained glass, sterling silver jewelry, pewter, applehead dolls, lamp shades, quilts, wrought iron, hand-knitted items, and puppets. Demonstrations of marquetry, backstrap weaving, painting on eggs, leather, calligraphy, chair caning, blacksmithing, pipe carving, soapstone carving, knitting, quilting, braiding, pottery, chain-saw art, spinning, and stenciling. Entertainment. Food available. 6,000 visitors annually. Admission free. **Directions:** From Interstate 89 exit 12 or 12A, go south on Route 11; the school is 4½ miles from either exit. (603) 763-5839.

WEST CAMPTON

New Hampshire Home Craft Cooperative, Inc., Route 3 (c/o Secretary, Campton, 03223). Amateur. Selections include rugs, woodwork, aprons, note paper, sweaters, mittens, pillowcases, ceramics, dolls, doll clothes, and doll furniture. Items cost 50¢ to $100 and up. Crafts are the work of members of the cooperative, who come from all parts of the state.

Open mid-June through mid-October, daily 9:30 to 5. **Directions:** From Interstate 93 exit 28, take Route 49 to West Campton, then turn left (south) on Route 3. (603) 726-8626.

Covered stoneware jar, River Bend Pottery (John Baymore), Wilton

To get to Wilton, take Route 3 north to exit 7W. Take Route 101A west to Route 101, then follow Route 101 west.

WILTON

Frye's Measure Mill, junction of Davisville Road and Burton Highway, 03086. Professional. Shop specializes in colonial and Shaker pantry box reproductions, brides' boxes, piggins, firkins, hand-painted boxes, paper cuttings, unusual hand-sewn clothes, and dolls. Prices range from $3 to $50. Unusual crafts are displayed here in an historic water-powered mill.

Open Memorial Day to Christmas, Thursday through Sunday 10 to 4. **Directions:** From Main Street in Wilton, take Route 31 toward Lyndeboro for 1½ miles; then bear left at the fork and travel another 1½ miles to the shop, which is on the right. (603) 654-6581.

River Bend Pottery (John Baymore), Old Mill and Intervale roads (RFD 2), 03086. Professional. Studio specializes in limited-production stoneware kitchen utensils and distinctive dinnerware sets. Offerings include one-of-a-kind vessels, sculptured pots, mugs, steamers, casseroles, baking dishes, vases, planters, and platters. Prices range from $4 to $300. This is a working studio; the display area is not separated from the work space, and visitors are encouraged to wander about and ask questions.

Open all year, by chance or appointment. **Directions:** Take Route 101 west through Wilton. About .1 mile past the Wilton Recycling Center, turn left onto Intervale Road. The studio sign is on the left, about ½ mile ahead. (603) 654-9404.

WOLFEBORO

Hampshire Pewter Company, Route 28, 03894. Professional. This is the only American source of Queen's Metal pewter, and there are just two others in the world. Queen's Metal is the highest grade and most durable type of pewter. Prices range from $9 to $269. "Most pewter is spun. Ours is completely hand cast and hand turned, the way pewter was made hundreds of years ago."

Open all year. Shop: Monday through Friday 9 to 3; showroom: Monday through Saturday 9 to 5. **Directions:** Take Interstate 93 exit 9N, then follow Route 28 north about 50 miles. (603) 569-4944.

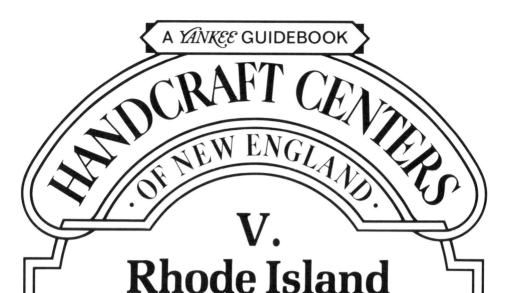

HANDCRAFT CENTERS

·OF NEW ENGLAND·

V.
Rhode Island

In Rhode Island, you have a wide choice of handcraft routes: you can follow the shoreline from Charlestown to Wickford (including, of course, a few short detours); you can concentrate on a group of crafts shops in Greater Providence or in Warwick; you can plan your outing to coincide with one of the state's regularly slated crafts festivals — or you can start from virtually any point on the Ocean State map and find a crafts outlet practically right next door.

One word of warning is in order here, however: many of the crafts outlets in Rhode Island are the studios of individual craftspeople who have additional jobs or sometimes leave their studios to attend crafts shows. So before you spend hours driving to reach an individual studio, please do take a minute or two to call and make an appointment with the craftsperson. The aggravation you save may be your own!

Antique-doll reproduction by Marilyn Ainsworth, MJA Porcelain Dolls, Hope Valley

BLOCK ISLAND

Ragged Sailor, Water Street, 02807. Professional and amateur. Shop features locally made, functional wrought-iron sculpture; porcelain goblets, vases, lamps, and plates; blown glass; and early-American-style doll house furniture. Prices range from $5 to $300. Products are carefully chosen for quality and variety; the shop is located in a Victorian building with an art gallery upstairs.

Open month of June, weekends 10 to 5; July through Labor Day, daily 9:30 to 5:30; day after Labor Day to Thanksgiving, weekends 10 to 5. **Directions:** Take the ferry to Block Island. The shop is on the main street, directly across from the Point Judith ferry dock in Old Harbor. (401) 466-7704.

CHARLESTOWN

The Fantastic Umbrella Factory, Route 1A, 02813. Professional. Selections include pottery from dinnerware to flower vases; stained and blown glass; woven goods; leather work; semiprecious-stone jewelry; brass, silver, gold, and feather jewelry; and macramé. All pieces are created by local craftspeople. Prices range from $2 to $200. The Fantastic Umbrella Factory is located in a complex of three buildings built between 1790 and 1870, two of which house crafts for sale.

Open mid-June through Labor Day, daily 10 to 6; day after Labor Day to Thanksgiving, Wednesday through Sunday 10 to 5; day after Thanksgiving to Christmas, daily 10 to 6; January through March, Thursday through Sunday 10 to 5; April through mid-June, Wednesday through Sunday 10 to 5. **Directions:** From Route 1 in town, take the Naval Air Station exit. The complex is ½ mile ahead on the right, on the ocean side of the street. (401) 364-6616.

"Essex," wooden ship model by Lawrence McCarthy, Cranston

CRANSTON

Lawrence McCarthy, 111 Tomahawk Trail, 02909. Professional. McCarthy specializes in wooden models of colonial (especially Revolutionary War) period ships, built to scale; models average three feet in length. Restoration work also done. Prices range from $1,500 to $10,000. McCarthy pays close attention to detail, and is expert in researching the period of each ship·

Open by appointment only; please call. (401) 943-3412.

CUMBERLAND

Jeeyls Country Store, 4116 Mendon Road, 02864. Professional and amateur. Selections include paintings, kitchen witches, painted slates, pottery, pin cushions, tooth-fairy pillows, dolls, baby items, aprons, holiday ornaments, handbags, decorated brooms, baskets, mats, and stuffed toys. Prices range from $2 to $35.

Open all year, Tuesday through Sunday 10 to 5. **Directions:** Take Interstate 95 south to Interstate 295 south. From Interstate 295, take Route 122 north. The store is 3 miles north of the exit, on the west side of the road. (401) 767-3560.

EAST PROVIDENCE

East Bay Ceramics, 30 James Street, 02914. Professional. Shop specializes in ceramics, including music and jewelry boxes, and lamps. Pieces are available both in finished form and in unfinished form for painting by customer. Prices range from 25¢ to $45. All work is hand crafted by shop owner Dolores Silva, who stresses high quality in her work.

Open all year, Monday through Friday 10 to 4, Saturday 11 to 3. **Directions:** Take Interstate 95 exit for Route 44. James Street is off Route 44; the shop is across from the city hall. (401) 438-6019.

FOSTER CENTER

Welcome Rood Studio, South Killingly Road, 02825. Professional. Studio features functional stoneware made on the premises, and also carries weaving, pillows, wall hangings, clothing, puppets, blown glass, forged-iron works, and spinning wool. Prices range from $5 to $75. Stoneware pottery is hand thrown in the shop adjacent to the salesroom, which was originally a general store and tavern built in the 1820s by Welcome Rood.

Open March through December, Friday through Sunday 1 to 5, and by appointment. **Directions:** From Providence, take Route 6 west, and turn south onto Route 94. The studio is 2 miles ahead, on the corner of Route 94 and South Killingly Road. (401) 397-3045.

HARMONY

Country Art, Phillips Lane (Box 63), 02829. Professional and amateur. Shop owner Linda Brook Baxter specializes in miniature reproductions of eighteenth- and nineteenth-century boxes, including wedding boxes. All boxes are hand painted, many in American folk-art styles. Also features plaques and welcome signs. Prices range from $1.50 to $185.

Open by appointment only; please call. (401) 949-0767.

HOPE VALLEY

MJA Porcelain Dolls, Sunset Drive, 02832. Professional. The Ainsworths create reproductions of both antique and modern dolls, and also make doll furniture, clothes, and accessories. Prices range from $2 to $200.

Open all year, daily 10 to 6. **Directions:** Heading south on Interstate 95, take exit 3B to Route 138. Follow Route 138 to Sunset Drive. (401) 539-2209.

KINGSTON

Fayerweather Craft Center, Moorisfield Road (Box 206, West Kingston, 02892). Professional and amateur. Selections include painted slates, hooked rugs, macramé, knitted goods, crocheted animals, quilling, embroidery, and hand-woven items. Pieces cost 75¢ to $25 and up.

Open May through December, Monday and Saturday 10 to 2; other times by appointment. **Directions:** Take Interstate 95, or Route 1 or 2, then head east on Route 138. Fayerweather is at the junction of routes 138 and 108. (401) 789-9072.

Antique-bisque-doll reproduction by Marilyn Ainsworth, MJA Porcelain Dolls, Hope Valley

NEWPORT

The Spectrum of American Artists and Craftsmen, Inc., Bannister's Wharf, 02840. Professional. Selections include pottery, graphics, ceramics in stoneware and porcelain, jewelry, weaving, soft sculptures, wood, enamels, leather work, blown glass, contemporary art glass, leaded glass, silk-screened items, and paintings. Prices range from $1 to $1,200. "We feature many unique, individually developed crafts, such as one steady line of fiber glass sculpture."

Open all year, daily 10 to 5:30. **Directions:** From Interstate 95, take Route 138 east to downtown. Follow signs to the harbor front, then to Bannister's Wharf. (401) 847-4477.

NORTH KINGSTOWN

Nancy Sevene, 440 South County Trail, 02852. Professional. Sevene specializes in decorative eggs, using original designs both inside and out. She also creates dough-art holiday decorations, and cornucopiae and basket work using fabrics and velvet ribbons. Prices range from 50¢ to $6.50.

Open by appointment only; please call. (401) 294-6267.

To get to Pascoag, take Interstate 295 to Route 44, then take Route 44 west to Chepachet. From Chepachet, take Route 100 north to Pascoag.

PASCOAG

Lee Menard, Buck Hill Road (RFD 1, Box 436), 02859. Professional. Featured are free-form mirrors created using clay and feathers — the original works of craftsperson Lee Menard. She also carries napkin rings, "mug mugs" (mugs with faces), weed pouches, and dried-flower arrangements. Prices range from 75¢ to $18. Menard stresses that her use of clay and feathers in combination is unique.

Open by appointment only; please call. (401) 568-6781.

Potter's Wheel, 9 Fairbanks Avenue, 02859. Professional. Shop specializes in pottery, including stoneware with a basic off-white glaze, decorated in patterns of wheat and cat-o'-nine-tails. Items featured include plates, casseroles, jars, lamps, and lanterns. Prices range from $5 to $60.

Open all year, Monday through Saturday; please call for appointment and directions. (401) 568-7471.

PEACE DALE

Lucinda Mellor-Neale, 72 Church Street, 02883. Studio features functional earthenware pottery, including dinnerware and kitchen accessories. Items include honey pots, coffee and tea cups, wine goblets, canisters, and mixing bowls. Prices range from $3.50 to $35. Mellor-Neale incorporates a traditional English style into her work.

Open all year, by appointment only. **Directions:** From Kingston, take Route 108 south approximately 2½ miles, bear left onto Columbia Street, then take the first left, onto Church Street. Shop is the first house on the left. (401) 783-3273.

To get to Providence, take Interstate 95 or Interstate 195.

PROVIDENCE

Nancy Rice, 36 Stadden Street, 02907. Professional. Rice specializes in hand-crafted jewelry, especially pendants, using natural stones set in silver. Prices range from $6 to $50. Rice uses "first quality stones" in her jewelry.

Open by appointment only; please call. (401) 461-7524.

The Opulent Owl, 295 South Main Street, 02903. Professional and amateur. A specialty here is pottery, the work of craftspeople from Maine to California. Hand-crafted jewelry is also sold. Prices range from $15 to $100.

Open all year, Monday through Saturday 10 to 5:30. **Directions:** From Boston, take Interstate 95 to Interstate 195 to downtown Providence exit. At the first traffic light, turn right onto South Water Street, and continue to a large parking lot in the rear of the shop. Heading north on Interstate 195, take the South Main Street exit. (401) 521-6698.

Perceptions, 806 Hope Street, 02906. Professional. Featured are the works — in all media — of more than seventy-five craftspeople and artists. Pieces include jewelry, glass, metal, baskets, wood, porcelain, fiber, and batik. Prices range from $10 to $1,000.

Open all year, Tuesday through Saturday 10 to 6. **Directions:** Take Interstate 95 exit for downtown Providence, and continue on the exit road to the first traffic light. Turn left onto East Avenue (which becomes Hope Street), and go about 1½ miles. The shop is on the right, directly across from Cinerama Theater. (401) 521-0370.

South Main Street Harvest Festival, South Main Street. 2-day juried show, sponsored by South Main Street Merchants Association (The Opulent Owl, 295 South Main Street, 02903) and held the third weekend in October. Hours: 10 to 6. About 75 professional and amateur exhibitors display many crafts, including pottery, jewelry, stained glass, soft sculpture, leather crafts, and musical instruments. Food available. Admission free. **Directions:** From Boston, take Interstate 95 to Interstate 195 to downtown Providence exit. At the first traffic light, turn right onto South Water Street, and continue to a large parking lot in the rear of The Opulent Owl shop. Heading north on Interstate 195, take the South Main Street exit. (401) 521-6698.

SCITUATE

Scituate Arts Festival, Route 116. A 3-day juried show, held during Columbus Day weekend. Hours: 10 to 7. Approximately 200 professional and amateur craftspeople and artists exhibit their work. Paintings are the main attraction, representing artists from many states. Crafts include wood, leather work, pottery, and stained glass. Leather and pottery techniques are demonstrated. Food available. 60,000 visitors annually. Admission free. **Directions:** From Providence or Interstate 295, head west on Route 6 to Route 116. The festival is held in front of an old, white, restored Congregational church. (401) 949-0767.

WAKEFIELD

Stone Tower Pottery, 145 Post Road, 02879. Professional. Owner Thomas Ladd specializes in hand-thrown functional stoneware pottery, including dinner sets, umbrella stands, jardinières, clocks, and bowls. Ladd uses a variety of glazes and colors, and limits his production to high-quality pieces. Custom work accepted. Prices range from $5 to $250.

Open all year, Monday through Friday 9 to 5; please call for directions. (401) 783-8923.

To get to Warwick, take Interstate 95 exit 10 onto Route 117 east, then follow signs.

WARWICK

Bellows by Soucy, 1532 West Shore Road, 02889. George Soucy specializes in hand-crafted turtle-back bellows, using basswood, rust deer lamb leather, brass tacks, and solid brass nozzles. All pieces are carefully hand finished. Prices range from $40 to $65.

Open by appointment only; please call. (401) 737-3513.

Jeri Kaplan, 6 Cedar Pond Drive #7, 02886. Professional. Kaplan specializes in hand-fired, enamel-on-copper jewelry; also carries plates, ashtrays, pictures, and adjustable belts with enameled buckles. Prices range from $5 to $50. All pieces are original in design — "no two are exactly alike."

Open by appointment only; please call. (401) 821-4138.

WEST WARWICK

Claudia Fay McConaghy, 3 Greenbush Road, 02893. Professional. McConaghy's specialty is soft-sculpture dolls, and dolls with music boxes inside them. Prices range from $6 to $20. McConaghy incorporates much detail into her creations, using quality materials and hand embroidering doll faces.

Open by appointment only; please call. (401) 822-1668.

To get to Wickford, take Route 1 or Route 1A.

WICKFORD

Different Drummer, 7 West Main Street, 02852. Professional. Shop features the works of over forty potters, who offer both functional and whimsical stoneware and porcelain such as oil lamps, music boxes, planters, and mirrors. Also carries stained-glass hangings and mirrors, wooden toys, mobiles, chimes, fine jewelry, batik hangings and prints, and candles. Prices range from $2 to $500.

Open all year, daily 10 to 6. **Directions:** The shop is on Route 1A in the village of Wickford, which is in the town of North Kingstown. (401) 294-4867.

Wickford Art Festival, Route 1A. A 3-day juried event, sponsored by the Wickford Art Association (580-10 Rod Road, North Kingstown, 02852) and held Friday through Sunday of the second weekend in July. Hours: 10 to 8. About 350 professional and amateur craftspeople and artists display and sell their works. Crafts include stained glass, jewelry, leather work, pottery, and woodcarving; artwork featured includes oil and acrylic paintings, water colors, sculpture, metalwork, portraiture, and photography. 100,000 visitors annually. Admission free. **Directions:** The festival site is 17 miles south of Providence; watch for festival signs at the rotary. (401) 294-3086.

WOONSOCKET

Autumnfest, World War II Park, Social Street. 3-day juried event, sponsored by the Greater Woonsocket Chamber of Commerce (Marquette Way, 02895) and held the second weekend of October. Hours: 10 to 10. About 75 professional and amateur exhibitors display a wide variety of crafts; most are demonstrated. Family activities are held, including contests and races. Food available. 100,000 visitors annually. Admission free. **Directions:** Permanent signs for the festival are posted throughout the town. (401) 762-1730.

Enamel-on-copper belt buckle by Jeri Kaplan, Warwick

Fresh Air, 18 High Street, 02895. Professional and amateur. Selections include handmade stationery; children's clothes and toys; hand-wrought sterling silver, gold, brass, and ceramic jewelry; and functional and decorative pottery. Most prices are under $20. The works of New England artisans are featured.

To get to Woonsocket, take Interstate 295 to Route 122, then follow Route 122 north.

Open all year, Monday through Saturday 10 to 5; plus Thursday to 6. **Directions:** The shop is on Route 122 in the center of town, opposite the renovated depot. (401) 765-2160.

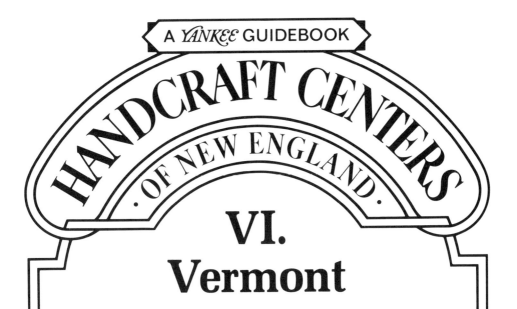

VI.
Vermont

Vermont has its share of crafts cooperatives and, in such tourist centers as Wilmington and Woodstock, a number of crafts shops fairly close together. But it is still a state of traditional Yankee independence, and there is absolutely no mathematical correlation between the quality of crafts sold at a shop, and the store's proximity to Interstate 89. (One of the most highly regarded crafts centers in the area is the Vermont State Craft Center at Frog Hollow in Middlebury — located at the intersection of several major routes, but far from any high-speed thruway.) So don't let the isolation of some of these shops from other crafts centers keep you from investigating their wares; just plan your visit for a day when you can travel leisurely along some of Vermont's back roads and enjoy the natural beauty that brought the craftspeople here before you.

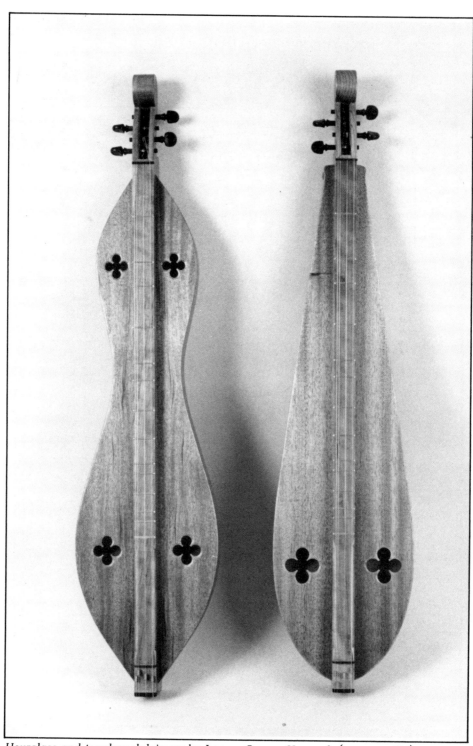

Hourglass and teardrop dulcimers by Jeremy Seeger, Hancock (see page 151)

ASCUTNEY

Ascutney Forge, Route 5, 05030. Professional. Shop sells fireplace accessories, spiral stairs, weather vanes, furniture, signs, hinges, brackets, and latches — custom designs. Prices range from $1.50 to $12,000. Emphasizes creativity in one-of-a-kind items, all handmade; "most items carry lifetime guarantees."

Open all year, Monday through Friday 7:30 to 4:30; also open some Saturdays — call ahead. **Directions:** Take Interstate 91 exit 8, and go one mile north on Route 5; the shop is on the right side of the road. (802) 674-5606.

Woodcarving by Boggis, routes 5 and 131 (Old Church Road, Claremont, NH 03743). Professional. Shop offers woodcarvings of all kinds, including six-foot cigar-store Indians; also small figures, eagles, and walking-stick heads. Custom work is a specialty. Pieces cost $10 to $3,000 and up. Store features high- and low-relief and three-dimensional carving; shop is unique "in that this is a full-time woodcarving operation, similar to those of the old-time woodcarvers."

Open all year, Monday through Friday 8 to 3:30, Saturday to noon. Finished work may be seen by appointment at Claremont, New Hampshire, address. **Directions:** The shop is at the junction of routes 5 and 131. (802) 674-2486 days, (603) 542-5618 evenings.

To get to Ascutney, take Interstate 91 exit 8, then head north on Route 5.

Stained glass, The Silk Purse and the Sow's Ear, Bethel

BELLOWS FALLS

Big Red Barn, Route 5 (Box 534), 05101. Professional and amateur. Selections include dried and silk-flower arrangements, hand-thrown pottery, ceramics, and wood burnings. Items cost $2 to $50 and up. Shop is located in a 150-year-old barn where the crafts are displayed among antiques and collectibles.

Open January through March, Wednesday through Monday 10 to 4; April through June, daily 9 to 5; July through December, daily 9 to 6. **Directions:** Heading north on Interstate 91, take exit 5 (Bellows Falls) and then go north on Route 5 for 2 miles. Or, heading south on Interstate 91, take exit 6 (Rockingham), then go south on Route 5 for 6 miles. (802) 463-3265.

BENNINGTON

Hawkins House, 262 North Street, 05201. Professional. Selections include hand-woven goods, jewelry, pottery, glass, leather, wood, and wrought iron. Prices range from $4 to $2,000, with most between $20 and $50. Claims "the largest selection of hand-woven clothing in southern Vermont."

Open May through December, daily 10 to 5:30,

Sunday from noon; January through April, same hours but closed Sunday. **Directions:** From junction of routes 7 and 9 in Bennington, go ¼ mile north on Route 7 to the traffic light at County Street. The shop is on the corner of County and North streets. (802) 447-0488.

To get to Bethel, take Interstate 89 exit 3, then head west on Route 107 to Route 12.

BETHEL

The Featherstitch Quilter (Box 93), 05032. Professional. Shop sells quilts in crib, twin, regular, queen, and king sizes; soft sculpture; tote bags in patchwork; and wall hangings. Prices range from $35 to $300.

Open all year, by appointment only. (802) 234-5010.

The Silk Purse and the Sow's Ear, routes 12 and 107 (Box 169), 05032. Professional. Selections include kaleidoscopes, brontosaurus planters, leather backpacks, quilts, paper cuttings, pottery, porcelain, sterling silver, weavings, and ironwork. Shop also offers custom furniture making, restoration, and repair. Prices range from $1 to $500. "We will assist you with design, color, and size."

Open daily all year, Monday through Saturday 9 to 5, Sunday and evenings by appointment. **Directions:** The shop is 2½ miles from Interstate 89 exit 3, at the junction of routes 12 and 107. (802) 234-5368.

To get to Brattleboro, take Interstate 91 exit 1, 2, or 3.

BRATTLEBORO

Body and Sole Leather, 22 High Street, 05301. Professional and amateur. Shop features shearling hats, vests, mittens, and slippers made on the premises; also carries hand-knit sweaters and hand-woven shawls, scarves, and tops made of natural fibers. Leather and sheepskin garments can be made to order. Prices range from $3 to $450.

Open all year, Monday through Saturday 9:30 to 5:30. **Directions:** The shop is downtown, two miles east of Interstate 91 exit 2. (802) 257-1174.

Dianne Shapiro, 19 Cedar Street, 05301. Professional. Studio specializes in soft-sculpture people representing a variety of professions and sports, crafted entirely by the studio owner; Shapiro also makes some soft animal toys. Prices range from $10 to $400. "No one else is producing soft sculpture in the style of mine, but it is the humor my work expresses that truly sets it apart."

Open by appointment only. (802) 254-4439.

L.J. Serkin Company, 51 Elliot Street, 05301. Professional. Shop features the works of eighty craftspeople, mostly from the local area; selections include forged jewelry by Tim Grannis, wooden bowls by Alan Stirt, pottery by Malcolm Wright, and woven place mats by Trudy Walker. Prices range from $4 to $200. The Serkin Company emphasizes crafts with high aesthetic value. There is a weaving studio on the premises.

Open all year, Monday through Saturday 9:30 to 5:30, Friday to 9. **Directions:** From Interstate 91 exit 2, take Route 9 to Main Street. Turn right onto Main Street, then right again onto Elliot Street. (802) 257-7044.

BRIDGEWATER

Brindalwood ... a Craft Shop, Bridgewater Mill Mall, Route 4 (Box 44), 05034. Professional. Selections include music boxes, jewelry, stained glass, honey pots, stoneware, porcelain, pewter, oil lamps, and blown and pressed glass. Prices range from $2 to $300, with most between $5 and $25. The shop is located in a converted woolen mill that is a national historic site. All items for sale here are made by American, primarily New England, craftspeople. Owner Marty Becktell's jewelry workshop is located in Brindalwood.

To get to Bridgewater, take Interstate 89 exit 1, then follow Route 4 west.

Open all year, Monday through Saturday 10 to 5, Sunday from noon. **Directions:** From Route 7 in Rutland, go 22 miles east on Route 4. From interstates 89 and 91, exit onto Route 4 and go west 12 miles. (802) 672-5144.

Vermont Clock Craft, Bridgewater Mill Mall, 05034. Professional. Shop specializes in wooden clocks made on the premises by one clock maker; selections include wall, mantle, grandfather, and grandmother clocks made in oak, cherry, walnut, pine, birch, butternut, and curly and bird's-eye maple. Prices range from $49 to $1,100.

Open all year, Monday through Saturday 10 to 4:30. **Directions:** The Bridgewater Mill Mall is on Route 4, on the left side of the road when you are heading west. (802) 672-3456.

Star-cluster pendant by Luella Schroeder, The Craft Shop at Molly's Pond, Cabot

CABOT

The Craft Shop at Molly's Pond, Route 2, 05647. Professional and amateur. Shop features a large line of sterling silver and gold jewelry by co-owner Luella Schroeder. Also sells blown glass, woodblock prints, ceramics, weaving, and paper items, all made by Vermont craftspeople. Prices range from 50¢ to $300.

Open month of May, Monday through Saturday 1 to 5:30; June through August, Monday through Saturday 10:30 to 5:30; September through December, Monday through Saturday 1 to 5:30. **Directions:** The shop is located on Route 2, approximately 2½ miles west of West Danville and 9 miles east of Marshfield.

COLCHESTER

Indian Brook Pottery, Bay Road (RD 5, Route 127),

147

Clay music box, Rah Earth, East Arlington

05446. Professional. Martha Burton Jones sells her own primitive pit-fired pottery: large floor vases, weed pots, and covered jars; also offers functional stoneware with natural wood-ash glazes, plus soap dishes, tea sets, canisters, casseroles, and oil lamps. Custom work accepted. Prices range from $5 to $200. Because this is a retail shop in a home and studio, there is the opportunity to meet the craftsperson and to ask questions concerning her production of handmade pottery.

Open all year, daily 9 to 6. **Directions:** From Interstate 89 exit 17, go south 2 miles on Route 7. The shop is 5 miles north of Burlington, just off Route 7 at the corner of Route 127. (802) 879-1641.

CONCORD

Mountaine Meadows Potterie (RFD, Box 68), 05824. Professional. Shop specializes in hand-thrown pottery for the kitchen and other areas of the home. Items for sale include mugs, pitchers, cream-and-sugar sets, jugs, cookie jars, lamps, bathroom sets, and mirrors. Prices range from $3.50 to $80. The pottery is decorated using individually carved wooden stamps that are pressed into the clay while it is still damp. Visitors are welcome to watch the pottery-making process.

Open all year, Monday through Friday 8:30 to 4:30. **Directions:** From Saint Johnsbury, take Route 2 east past the intersection with Route 18; go through East Saint Johnsbury, then turn left at Don's Wayside Furniture. After 1½ miles turn right onto a dirt road; go 1 mile to the red barn (shop) marked by a sign. (802) 748-9242.

CRAFTSBURY

Antiques and Uniques Festival, Craftsbury common. 1-day crafts festival, sponsored by the Vermont Children's Aid Society (72 Hungerford Terrace, Burlington, 05401) and held the second Saturday in July. Hours: 10 to 5. About 115 professional and amateur craftspeople exhibit wrought iron, pottery, jewelry, spinning, weaving, and wooden ware. Demonstrations of some crafts. Antiques are also shown. Approximately 2,500 visitors annually. Admission free. **Directions:** From Interstate 89, take exit 7 to Barre, then head north on Route 14 to Craftsbury (about 25 miles). The common is off Route 14. (802) 864-9883.

DERBY LINE

Tranquil Things, 43 Main Street (Box 338), 05830. Professional. Selections include wood, glass, pottery, and textiles. Prices range from 50¢ to $270. "We try to carry things that are unusual, things that are beautiful, and things that are beneficial to people to have. We are a store for presents — for oneself or for others."

Open all year, Monday through Saturday 10 to 5; extended hours in summer and before Christmas. **Directions:** The shop is close to the Derby Line exit from Interstate 91, in the residential district, south of the business district. (802) 873-3454.

EAST ARLINGTON

Rah Earth, Candle Mill Village, Old Mill Road, 05252. Professional. Shop specializes in pottery made on the premises, including potpourri pots, fountains, oil lamps, clocks, music boxes, and egg separators. Also carries stained glass, leather, macramé, jewelry, and lamps. Special orders accepted. Prices range from 40¢ to $400. Visitors may watch pottery being made.

To get to East Arlington, take Route 7 to Arlington, then follow signs.

Open January through May, Wednesday through Monday noon to 5; June through December, Monday through Saturday 10 to 5:30, Sunday from noon. **Directions:** From Arlington, take East Arlington Road to Ice Pond Farm Road; turn right and follow Ice Pond Farm Road to Candle Mill Village. The shop is upstairs in the first building. (802) 375-6522.

The Village Peddler, Old Mill Road, 05252. Professional and amateur. Selections include hand-crafted cradles, custom-made furniture and frames, handmade quilts, dolls, doll-house furniture, pewter figurines, original stained glass, and pottery. Prices begin at $2. Features products crafted by New Englanders. "We design and build furniture to customer specifications, and we do custom framing. We run an old-time country shop with old-time friendliness."

Open all year, daily 9 to 5:30. **Directions:** Take Route 7 north to Arlington, then turn right at the sign for East Arlington and go 1 mile to The Village Peddler. Or take Route 313 from Cambridge, New York, to Route 7A. Turn right onto Route 7A, then left onto East Arlington Road, then right onto Old Mill Road and go ½ mile to the shop. (802) 375-6443.

EAST BURKE

Vermont Sheep and Wool Festival, Darling Hill Road. 1-day crafts fair, sponsored by Friends of Burklyn/Vermont Sheepbreeders Association (Box 15, West Burke, 05871) and held the third Saturday in May. Hours: 9 to 4:30. About 20 professional and amateur craftspeople exhibit such wool-related crafts as weaving, knitting, and spinning; a fleece-to-shawl spinning competition is held; handmade shawls are auctioned; and much more. Demonstrations of shearing, spinning, and weaving. 1,000 visitors annually. Admission free. **Directions:** Take Interstate 91 exit 23, and follow Route 5 north through Lyndonville to Route 114; turn right onto Route 114 and go ½ mile to the first left, then 3 miles to Burklyn Barns. (802) 467-3262, or 467-3460.

EAST HAVEN

Elin K. Paulson, Lost Nation Road, 05837. Professional. Shop specializes in stained-glass flowers, faces, symmetricals, and improvisations. Prices range from $5 to $500.

Open by appointment only. (802) 467-3997.

EAST TOPSHAM

Willy Hill Pottery and Baskets, Willy Hill Road (RFD 2, Groton, 05046). Professional. Shop specializes in baskets for home, garden, travel, and picnics. Also functional pottery — dinnerware, tableware, and accessories. Prices range from $7 to $120 for baskets, $6 to $80 for pottery. Says basket weaver Jackie Speeter Abrams, "I strive to make the baskets functional — and also to make them look different from imported baskets." Steven Abrams' pottery features a crystal blue glaze.

Open all year, by appointment only. (802) 439-6265.

GLOVER

Northeast Kingdom Center for Handweaving Studies, Main Street (Star Route, Barton, 05822). Professional. Studio offers a wide range of products, all hand woven by the owner, Kate Butler; items include everything from shawls to bedspreads. Prices range from $3.75 to $300. Butler specializes in reproductions of colonial fabrics, reflecting our colonial heritage.

Open daily all year, "but call ahead as I frequently do craft shows." **Directions:** Take Interstate 91 exit 25 in Barton, and go 1½ miles south on Route 16 to Glover. (802) 525-6695.

GRAFTON

Thistledown Gallery, 05146. Professional. Gallery features paintings, pottery, quilts, Christmas ornaments, and ceramics. Prices range from $2.50 to $425.

Open June through October, Monday through Saturday 9 to 5. **Directions:** Take Interstate 91 exit 5, and follow Route 121 to Grafton. The gallery is alongside the Old Tavern. (802) 843-2340.

GREENSBORO

The Miller's Thumb (Box 98), 05841. Professional and amateur. Shop features Vermont handcrafts of all types, from one-of-a-kind pieces to production crafts. There are also some crafts from other states and countries. Prices range from 50¢ to $250. Shop is located in remodeled grist mill with a window in the floor, affording a view of the millstream below.

Open late June through mid-September, Monday and Wednesday through Saturday 10 to 5. **Directions:** Greensboro is off Route 16, approximately 23 miles northwest of Saint Johnsbury, and 5 miles north of Hardwick; the shop is in the center of the village. (802) 533-2960.

HANCOCK

Jeremy Seeger, Mountain Dulcimers, Fassett Hill (Box 117), 05748. Professional. Shop specializes in Appalachian mountain dulcimers made of mahogany and cherry, and hammered dulcimers made of maple. Prices range from $185 to $500. Seeger designs and builds instruments for superior sound and ease of playing.

Open daily all year, by appointment only. "Please phone or write ahead, especially in winter." (802) 767-3790.

HYDE PARK

Cooper Hill Quiltworks, Main Street (Drawer C), 05655. Professional. Shop specializes in hand-quilted comforters and wall hangings. Prices begin at $150. The Quiltworks carries "well-made items with vibrant colors and nice designs."

Open by appointment only. (802) 888-4497.

IRASBURG

Silver and Crafts, Jewelry and Gifts (Box 86), 05845. Professional. Shop features jewelry by owner Steffi V. Stackelberg; also some pottery, leather, toys, paintings, woodcut prints, and gift items — all handmade. Prices range from $5 to $125.

Open from the end of May through September, daily 9 to 5. "Sometimes closed, when I attend a show." **Directions:** From Interstate 91 exit 26, follow Route 58 west to Irasburg (about 5 miles). The shop is located at the junction of routes 58 and 14. (802) 754-6012.

JACKSONVILLE

Stone Soldier Pottery, Mill Hill, 05342. Professional. Shop features functional stoneware pottery handmade on the premises by Robert C. Burnell; also jewelry, weaving, blown glass, wood products, and other handcrafts. Prices range from $5 to $500.

Open all year, Monday through Saturday 10 to 5,

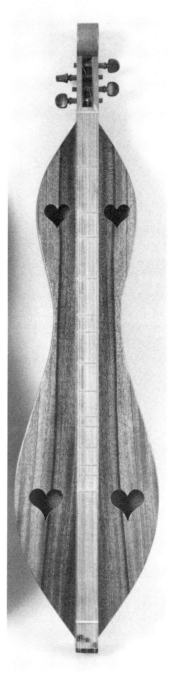

Hourglass dulcimer by Jeremy Seeger, Hancock

Sunday from noon. **Directions:** From Interstate 91 exit 2, head west on Route 9 to Wilmington, then south on Route 100 to Jacksonville. The shop is located in the village, just off Route 100. (802) 368-7077.

LUDLOW

Pottery Works, routes 100 and 103, 05149. Professional. Shop features a wide variety of functional stoneware made in the shop by owner Susan Wishnatzki; offers such items as candle holders, lamps, hanging planters, dinnerware, soup tureens, and platters. Custom orders accepted. Prices range from $2 to $50. "I market all of my products in this retail outlet. My colors are particularly bright for stoneware."

Open September through June, Wednesday through Monday 11 to 5; July and August, daily 11 to 6. **Directions:** The shop is on Route 103 at the base of Okemo Mountain in Ludlow. (802) 228-8743.

To get to Manchester and Manchester Center, take Interstate 91 exit 2 onto Route 9. Head west on Route 9 to Bennington, then take Route 7 north to Manchester, then Manchester Center. Or, take Route 30 or Route 11 to Manchester Center, then go south on Route 7 to Manchester. (Routes 7, 11, and 30 converge in Manchester Center.)

MANCHESTER

Southern Vermont Craft Fair, Manchester Recreation Area, Route 30. A 3-day juried crafts fair, sponsored by Craftproducers Markets, Inc. (North Hill, Readsboro, 05350) and held during the first weekend of August. Hours: Friday noon to 6, Saturday and Sunday 10 to 6. Approximately 100 craftspeople exhibit contemporary crafts, both utilitarian and non-functional; crafts for the kitchen and throughout the home, and crafts as fashions. Pottery is demonstrated. About 10,000 visitors annually. Admission charge for adults; children free. **Directions:** The Manchester Recreation Area is located north of town. (802) 423-7692.

MANCHESTER CENTER

Green Mountain Stained Glass, Factory Point Square (Box 831), 05255. Professional. Selections include stained-glass shades, boxes, and windows by owners Harlan Levey and Carol Jodlbauer; also pottery fish tanks and water fountains, hand-woven rugs, and handmade wall clocks. Prices range from $5 to $700.

Open all year, daily 10 to 5. **Directions:** The shop is on Route 7 in Factory Point Square. (802) 362-3612.

Herdsmen Leathers, Route 7 (Box 1072), 05255. Professional. Shop features sheepskin coats, jackets, and blazers; lambskin suedes; leather handbags, briefcases, date books, and footwear. Prices range from $3 to $800. "Our inventory comes mostly from individual craftspeople all over the country."

Open all year, Monday through Saturday 9:30 to 5:30, Sunday noon to 5. **Directions:** The shop is on the north edge of town on Route 7. (802) 362-2751.

MARLBORO

Applewoods', Route 9 (Box 66), 05344. Professional. Shop specializes in "aformal" furniture — coffee tables, benches, and dining tables. Also carries accessories such as turned bowls, vases, lamps, clocks, and mirrors. Pieces cost $25 to $2,000 and up. Features hardwoods from the area — maple, yellow birch, and cherry burls.

Open all year, daily 10 to 6. **Directions:** From Interstate 91 exit 2, go west 10 miles on Route 9. (802) 254-2908.

Lucy G. Serkin Handweaving, Town Hill Road, 05344. Professional. Shop specializes in hand-woven skirts, stoles, ponchos, and blankets. Prices range from $30 to $250. Emphasizes "quality, simplicity, and beauty, of course."

Open by appointment only. (802) 257-0181.

To get to Marlboro, take Interstate 91 exit 2 in Brattleboro, and head west on Route 9.

MIDDLEBURY

To get to Middlebury, take Route 7, 23, 125, or 30; all four converge in the town.

Cornwall Crafts, Route 30 (RD 2), 05753. Professional. Selections include handmade furniture in early American styles, woolen shawls, spinning wheels, hand-wrought ironware, pottery, rugs, hand-hooked chair pads, candles, mirrors, hangings, lamps, lamp shades, posters, cards, and batik hangings. Prices range from $3 to $700. Shop features "a unique combination of handcrafts and quality products of small manufacturers of furniture. We operate out of a 175-year-old barn surrounded by mountains and apple orchards."

Open November through May, Tuesday through Sunday 10 to 5:30; June through October, daily 10 to 6. **Directions:** The shop is on Route 30, just 3 miles south of the center of Middlebury. (802) 462-2438.

Vermont State Craft Center at Frog Hollow, 05753. Professional. Selections include stained glass, pottery, quilts, jewelry, rugs, hand-woven garments, shawls, blown glass, toys, and stuffed dolls. Prices range from $1 to $3,000. The center regularly features shows such as the Interior Show in March, Vermont Images in May, Summer Celebration in June, Multiples in September, and Things Made by Hand for Christmas in November.

Open February through April, Tuesday through Saturday 10 to 5; May through December, Monday through Saturday 10 to 5; closed January. **Directions:** The shop is in the center of town. (802) 388-4871.

Applehead doll, Cornwall Crafts, Middlebury

MONTGOMERY CENTER

Peter Bruce Gallery (Box 327), 05471. Gallery offers an amalgamation of crafts and art, fine arts and New England antiques displayed in a Victorian home. Crafts include sculptured porcelain, fiber wall hangings, appliqué paintings, batiks, soft sculptures, and wood-form sculptures. Prices range from $15 to $1,500. Crafts presented are actually art forms created from materials previously associated with functional crafts. Featured are "faces of old men and jolly imps, coaxed and carved from natural wood forms" by sculptor Bob Keegan.

Open all year, daily 10 to 10. **Directions:** Take Interstate 89 exit 10, onto Route 100. Go north through Stowe and Morrisville and into Eden; then take Route 118 west for 13 miles to town. (802) 326-4539.

MONTPELIER

Artisan's Hand Craft Store and Gallery Cooperative, Langdon Street, 05602. Professional. Shop features hand-woven and batik clothing, stained and blown glass, furniture, soft sculptures, jewelry, pottery, dolls, hammocks, and rugs. Prices range from $5 to $250. Cooperative membership is "limited to Vermont professionals whose work must be juried."

Open all year, Monday through Saturday 10 to 5. **Directions:** Langdon Street is off Main Street; the shop is within sight of the state capitol. (802) 229-9492.

NORTH DANVILLE

Pleasant View Arts and Crafts (RFD 2, Saint Johnsbury, 05819). Professional. Shop specializes in nature lamp shades, nature plaques, shades with oil paintings, and sculptured shades. Prices range from $10 to $45. All the natural objects used in the lamp shades are collected from the countryside surrounding the shop.

Open all year, Sunday through Friday 10 to 4; other times by appointment. **Directions:** Take Interstate 91 exit 21 and follow the North Danville road 2.4 miles. Turn left onto a dirt road, and go up the hill 1 mile to the first house on the left. (802) 748-2243.

NORWICH

Trillium Fine Crafts, 1820 House, Main Street (Box 504), 05055. Professional. Selections include ceramics, bronze bells, mobiles, multicolored canvas totes, unusual baby gifts, hand-silk-screened cards, and wooden containers. Also gold, silver, and ceramic jewelry; and hand-woven shawls, scarves, and floor pillows. Prices range from 50¢ to $125. Features both contemporary and traditional American handcrafts that are "not otherwise found in our area — some crafts are designed exclusively for the store."

Open all year, Monday through Saturday 10 to 5. **Directions:** Take Interstate 91 exit 13 (Norwich/Hanover) and head west onto Main Street. (802) 649-1658.

POULTNEY

The Craft Seller, 71 Main Street, 05764. Professional and amateur. Featured here are quilts, which can be made to order in any size; and soft-sculpture dolls, pillows, and hangings. Prices range from $1 to $150. A large variety of crafts is interspersed with over 100 bolts of calico fabrics and selected antiques.

Open all year, Monday through Saturday 10 to 5, except closed the week after Christmas. **Directions:** Heading west from Rutland on Route 4, take exit 4 onto Route 30. Head south on Route 30 to Poultney, about 7 miles. (802) 287-9713.

PROCTORSVILLE

Proctorsville Pottery and Weaving, Twenty Mile Stream Road (RFD 1, Box 10), 05153. Professional. Shop specializes in functional and decorative stoneware pottery, and items made from the wool of owners Alan and Wendy Regier's small flock of sheep. Prices range from $2 to $150. The shop is in a working barn, and the studios are open to the public. "Our studios are off the main highways and are very low key."

Open July through October 20, Wednesday through Monday 10 to 6; December through May, Sunday through Friday 10 to 3. **Directions:** From Interstate 91 exit 8, follow Route 131 west toward town. Look for Twenty Mile Stream Road; follow it for ¾ mile until you see a sign for the shop. (802) 226-7331.

PUTNEY

The Putney Woodshed, South Main Street, 05346. Professional and amateur. Shop features wood crafts by a variety of artists; items include one-of-a-kind wood turnings by Russ Zimmerman, sculptured containers by Deborah Bump, wood engravings by Randy Miller, and woodcuts by shop owner Margaret Torrey. Prices range from $2 to $75. The shop is "small, but full of an unusual collection of selected crafts, all made of natural materials, many by small producers from our region."

Open all year (except part of February), Monday and Wednesday through Saturday 10 to 5, Sunday from noon. **Directions:** Take Interstate 91 exit 4 onto Route 5, which is South Main Street. The shop is in a barn by a white house with blue shutters, opposite the credit union. (802) 387-4481.

SAINT JOHNSBURY

RAMA Enamels, 18 Summer Street (mailing address: West Danville, 05873). Professional. Shop specializes in enameled items such as jewelry, art objects, pictures, and switch plates, all made on the premises. Also carries selected crafts from other artisans. Prices range from $5 to $85. This is a family operation, with two generations of enamelists demonstrating their craft. Specialty items are available. "We make a large variety of enamels uniquely our own, as we are self-taught."

Open June through December, Monday through Saturday 10 to 5. **Directions:** Take Interstate 91 exit 21 toward Saint Johnsbury, and go one mile, then take a left up a steep hill. The RAMA Enamels studio is on the left and is marked by a sign. (802) 748-8558, or 563-2384 evenings.

SAINT JOHNSBURY CENTER

Fall Brook Pottery, 32 Main Street (Box 41), 05863. Professional. Shop specializes in distinctive handmade stoneware and porcelain, both "elegantly functional pieces and fantasy porcelain figures." Prices range from $1 to $150. Items for sale are made on the premises. The gallery hosts changing shows featuring the works of local craftspeople and artists.

Open January through April, Wednesday through Saturday 9 to 5; May through November, Monday through Saturday 9 to 5; month of December, Monday through Wednesday and Saturday 9 to 6, Thursday and Friday to 9. **Directions:** The shop is located on Route 5, 1½ miles north of Saint Johnsbury. (802) 748-5252.

SHAFTSBURY

The Magic Sleigh, Route 7A, 05262. Professional and amateur. Selections include Christmas gifts and crafts such as original oil paintings done on goose eggs, feather ornaments, ceramics, Renaissance angels made of draped papier mâché, and limited-edition porcelain-faced Santa dolls. Prices range from $3.25 to $450.

Open Memorial Day weekend through December 24, daily 10 to 5:30. **Directions:** From Interstate 91, take exit 2 in Brattleboro and head west on Route 9 to Bennington (about 40 miles). Then head north on Route 7 to Shaftsbury (about 7 miles), and look for signs to Route 7A. (802) 442-5397.

To get to Stowe, take Interstate 89 exit 10, then go north on Route 100.

STOWE

Beckerhoff, Ltd., Route 100 (Box 62), 05672. Professional. This is a full-service jewelry store with an emphasis on handmade jewelry. Prices range from $3 to $1,200.

Open all year, Monday through Saturday 10 to 6. **Directions:** The shop is on Route 100 in Stowe village. (802) 253-7668.

Samara, Mountain Road, Route 108, (Box 1115), 05672. Professional. Selections include jewelry in gold, silver, bronze, and bone; functional and artistic stoneware and porcelain; wrought iron; stained-glass mirrors and window hangings; custom-made quilts and wall hangings; woven lamps and pillows; candles; and wooden toys. Prices range from $1 to $200. Samara emphasizes variety and quality. "With very few exceptions, all of our items are hand-crafted in the United States, primarily in New England. We offer crafts by 250 artisans."

Open all year, Monday through Saturday 10 to 6, Sunday 11 to 5; early spring and late fall, closed Sunday. **Directions:** From Route 100 in Stowe, turn left onto Route 108. The craft gallery is 2 miles north of Stowe village, in the West Branch Shopping Center. (802) 253-8318.

The Stowe Pottery, Route 108 (Box 262), 05672. Professional. Shop specializes in pottery created on the premises, and also features pewter, blown glass, gold, silver, wood products, and weaving. Prices range from 75¢ to $750.

Open all year, Monday through Saturday 9:30 to 5. **Directions:** The shop is 100 yards from the intersection of routes 100 and 108, on Route 108 at the covered footbridge. (802) 253-4693.

Village Artisans, Pond Street (RD 2, Box 6460), 05672. Professional. Selections include hand-thrown pottery and sculptured porcelain; wooden bowls, plates, and toys; traditional and original windows and hangings in imported stained glass; ironwork; copper weather vanes; quilts; wall hangings; and soft sculptures. Prices range from $2 to $2,000. Featured in the shop is the work of seven professional craftspeople who are members of this cooperative endeavor.

Open all year, daily 10 to 5, except closed April, May, and November. **Directions:** The shop is one block behind Shaw's General Store; Pond Street is parallel to Main Street. (802) 253-8068.

Stoneware landscape jar by Gregory McNally, Fall Brook Pottery, Saint Johnsbury Center

---

STRATTON MOUNTAIN

Stratton Arts Festival, Base Lodge, Stratton Mountain Ski Area, 05155. A 1-month juried crafts fair, sponsored by Stratton Arts Festival, Inc., and held from mid-September through mid-October (during foliage season). Hours: daily 9:30 to 5. About 300 professional and amateur craftspeople and artists exhibit lithographs, woodcuts, prints, collages, photography, batiks, stoneware and porcelain pottery, quilts, soft sculptures, wooden ware, and silver and gold jewelry. Demonstrations of weaving, stained glass, batik, blown glass, doll making, pottery, wood carving, raku, and other crafts. 15,000 visitors annually. Admission charge. **Directions:** Take Route 30 from Brattleboro or Manchester to Stratton access road. (802) 297-2200.

THETFORD CENTER

R. Voake, Toymaker, Route 113, 05075. Professional. Shop features ridable wooden trucks and trains; rocking and rolling animals; Noah's arks; planes; building blocks; doll carriages and cribs; and adult toys including gum-ball machines, river boats, and molar mobiles. Prices range from $1.50 to $155. Voake offers approximately 125 different designs.

Open all year, daily 10 to 6. **Directions:** Heading north on Interstate 91, take exit 14 (Thetford). Turn left onto Route 113 toward Thetford Hill, and continue 4 miles. Watch for a sign on the right; the shop is on the left. (802) 785-2837.

UNDERHILL

Timothy Grannis, Silver/Goldsmith, North Underhill Road, 05489. Professional. Grannis specializes in contemporary designer jewelry — sculptural neckpieces, rings, bracelets, and earrings in silver and gold — all on display. Work is designed and executed by the artist in his studio, which is attached to the showroom. Wedding bands are done on commission. Prices range from $40 to $600. Showroom features "some of Vermont's finest metalworking in precious metals; my work is also sold in the best galleries in the Northeast."

Open all year, Monday through Friday 8 to 4:30. **Directions:** From Interstate 89, take exit 15 and follow Route 15 east through Underhill Flats. The studio/showroom is ½ mile off Route 15; the turnoff is marked by a sign. (802) 899-3750.

WAITSFIELD

Tree Top Shop and Wobbley Knees, Bridge Street (Box 43), 05673. Professional. Shops specialize in holiday ornaments and stuffed toys of all kinds for all ages. Featured are quilts, weaving, wooden ornaments, and mobiles. Prices range from $3 to $500. This is a family business offering original, signed designs.

Open all year, daily 10 to 5. **Directions:** The shops are just off Route 100, in the blue building next to the 1833 covered bridge. (802) 496-3997.

WEST DOVER

Mount Snow Craft Fair, Base Lodge, Mount Snow Ski Area. 3-day juried crafts fair, sponsored by Craftproducers Markets, Inc. (North Hill, Readsboro, 05350) and held during Columbus Day weekend. Hours: Saturday noon to 6, Sunday and Monday 10 to 6. About 75 craftspeople exhibit contemporary crafts, both utilitarian and non-functional: crafts for the kitchen and throughout the home, and crafts as fashions. A pleasant ambiance, with three floors of crafts to explore. 7,500 visitors annually. Admission charge for adults; children free. **Directions:** The ski area is on Route 100, about 10 miles north of Wilmington. (802) 423-7692.

WESTMORE

W. Robert Graham, Coppersmith, Willoughby Lake (Box 103C, RFD 2, Orleans, 05860). Professional. Shop specializes in hand-hammered copper vessels and utensils such as wine racks, log holders, candle snuffers, candle holders, and other, one-of-a-kind items in original designs. Prices range from $10 to $350.

Open June through September, Thursday through Sunday 2 to 5; other times by appointment. **Directions:** From Interstate 91, take exit 25 to Barton; then go about 9 miles east on Route 16 to Willoughby Lake. The shop is ½ mile east of Westmore Church. (802) 525-6647.

WHITE RIVER JUNCTION

North Country Shop and Gallery, Route 5, 05001. Professional and amateur. Shop features the work of 200 craftspeople and artists; includes pottery, blown glass, collectors' dolls, pewter, candles, porcelain, and water colors. Prices range from $1 to $1,000.

Open June through October, Monday through Saturday 9 to 9, Sunday 11 to 5; November and December, Monday through Saturday 9 to 9; January through May, Monday through Saturday 9 to 6. **Directions:** Take Interstate 91 exit 11 onto Route 5. The shop is located in the Howard Johnson complex. (802) 295-5500.

WILLIAMSTOWN

Knight's Small Cabinet Store, Spider Web Farm, Cliff Place, 05679. Professional. Shop features wooden accessories: lap desks, spider-web plaques, and jewelry boxes. Prices range from $7.95 to $150, with most under $50. Knight's is a one-person operation in which everything is handmade — the spider-web plaque "is unique and is our best-selling item."

Open January through April, weekends 9 to 6, weekdays by request; May through October, daily 9 to 6; November and December, weekends by appointment. **Directions:** Take Interstate 89 exit 5 and go 3 miles; turn right onto Route 14. The shop is just off Route 14, south of Williamstown Shopping Center. (802) 433-5568.

VERMONT

To get to Wilmington, take Interstate 91 exit 2 and go west on Route 9 for 20 miles. Or, take Route 9 east from Bennington for 20 miles.

WILMINGTON

Art on the Mountain, Haystack Mountain. 10-day juried crafts fair, sponsored by the Deerfield Valley Health Center Volunteers (Box 275, 05363), and held during the second two weeks of August. Hours: 10 to 5. Approximately 150 professional and amateur craftspeople and artists exhibit paintings, photography, sculpture, and other crafts in all media. Prices range from $2 to $2,000. About 3,800 visitors annually. Admission charge. **Directions:** From Wilmington traffic light, go north on Route 100 to Cold Brook Road. Follow Cold Brook Road to Haystack Mountain access road. (802) 464-8096.

Craft-Haus, Top of the Hill Road (Box 755), 05363. Professional. Shop features silver and gold cloisonné jewelry, one-of-a-kind signed pieces; enameled pendants; metal sculptures, especially decorative sunbursts; and Ted E. Bear houses made out of tree stumps, complete with bears and furnishings. Prices range from $2.50 to $500. All of the crafts are created by Ursula and Ed Tancrel. Talks on cloisonné and enameling are also offered.

Open all year (except closed in mud season), Saturday and Sunday 10 to 5, weekdays by chance and by appointment. **Directions:** Take Route 100 north 1½ miles from the Wilmington traffic light, and turn right onto Stowe Hill Road. Go 2 miles and turn right onto Top of the Hill Road. (802) 464-2164.

John McLeod, Ltd., West Main Street, 05363. Professional. Shop specializes in hand-crafted gourmet wooden ware such as cutting boards, knife racks, pot racks, lazy Susans, clocks, and wine racks. Prices range from $2 to $400. Work is done on the premises; visitors are welcome to watch the process.

Open all year, daily 8 to 6. **Directions:** The shop is on Route 9, just ½ mile west of the traffic light in Wilmington. (802) 464-8175.

Klara-Simpla, 10 Main Street, 05363. Professional and amateur. Shop specializes in flameware pottery such as skillets, cups, saucers, teapots, and coffee pots. Also wooden cups, bowls, and utensils. Prices range from $5 to $100. Crafts are confined to useful things.

Open all year, daily 10 to 6, except closed Thanksgiving and Christmas. **Directions:** The shop is located at the intersection of routes 100 and 9. (802) 464-5257.

Quaigh Design Centre, West Main Street, 05363. Professional. Selections include stained glass, stoneware and porcelain pottery, sterling silver and gold jewelry, lamps, lamp shades, and handmade cards. Prices range from $2 to $250.

Open all year, daily 10 to 6, except closed Thanksgiving and Christmas. **Directions:** The shop is located on Route 9, just west of the Wilmington traffic light. (802) 464-2780.

WINDSOR

Vermont State Craft Center, Windsor House, Main Street (Box 110), 05089. Professional. Shop features hand-built and hand-thrown pottery, blown glass, stained glass, quilts, macramé, rugs, wrought iron, lamp shades, prints, leather goods, jewelry, baskets, soft sculpture, and toys. Prices range from 40¢ to $1,500, with most under $50. The crafts are made by over 250 Vermont craftspeople.

Open all year, Monday through Saturday 10 to 5. **Directions:** The center is located on Route 5, between Interstate 91 exit 8 (Ascutney) and exit 9 (Hartland). (802) 674-6729.

WOODSTOCK

Ethier Stained Glass Studio, Route 4, 05091. Professional. Studio specializes in stained- and leaded-glass designs for windows, interior panels, lamps, sculptures, mirrors, and other home uses. Visitors are welcome to observe various stages of works in progress. All work is designed and executed by studio owner Linda Ethier.

Open all year, Tuesday through Saturday 9:30 to 5. **Directions:** The studio is 2 miles west of the Woodstock green. (802) 457-2354.

Unicorn, 15 Central Street, 05091. Professional and amateur. Selections include hand-crafted jewelry in 14-karat gold, sterling silver, enamel, brass, pearls, and precious and semiprecious stones; gold and silver Italian chains; pottery and porcelain for household functional and decorative use; wooden ware items featuring marquetry; cutting boards; rolling pins; woven place mats, napkins, rag rugs, and shawls; unicorns in every guise from jewelry to soft sculpture; silk-screened cards; and baskets. Prices range from 50¢ to $900. "We are constantly looking for and buying new and unique crafts, all of which are artistically displayed."

Open January through May, Monday through Saturday 9:30 to 5:30, and occasionally on Sunday; June through December, Monday through Saturday same hours, plus 11 to 4 on Sunday. **Directions:** The shop is in the heart of Woodstock village, on Route 4. (802) 457-2480.

Woodstock Summer Festival, on the green. 2-day juried crafts festival, sponsored by Pentangle Council on the Arts (Box 172, 05091) and held the weekend before or after the Fourth of July. Hours: 10 to 6. About 40 professional and amateur craftspeople exhibit crafts of all kinds. Demonstrations of porcelain, pottery, jewelry, pewter, weaving, and others. 2,000 visitors annually. Admission free. **Directions:** The green is on Route 4, in the center of Woodstock. (802) 457-3981.

To get to Woodstock, take Interstate 89 exit 1 onto Route 4 and follow signs approximately 10 miles to town.

Index of Craftspeople,
Shops, Events, and Event Sponsors

Index of Types of Crafts